PEOPLE OF THE SHINING MOUNTAINS

To Kristin, for her patience and understanding, and to Stephen, David, and Carrie.

THE · UTES · OF · COLORADO

PEOPLE OF THE SHINING MOUNTAINS

CHARLES S. MARSH

PRUETT **P**PUBLISHING COMPANY
Boulder, Colorado

Library of Congress Cataloging in Publication Data

Marsh, Charles S. (Charles Seabrooke), 1926-
    People of the shining mountains.

    Bibliography: p.
    Includes index.
    1. Ute Indians—History. I. Title.
E99.U8M37   978.8'00497   81-21032
ISBN 0-87108-620-4   AACR2
ISBN 0-87108-613-1 (pbk.)

First Edition

5   6   7   8   9

Printed in the United States of America

ACKNOWLEDGEMENTS

Special thanks is given to the Denver Public Library, the Aspen Public Library, the Colorado State Historical Society, the New Mexico Historical Library and Museum, the New Mexico State Archives, the Heye Museum of the American Indian, the U.S. Department of the Interior, and especially the Ute Tribal Councils and Museum.

PHOTO CREDITS

Photographs are used with the courtesy of the following sources: The American Museum of Natural History, New York, New York; pages 110, 115, and 151.

The Colorado State Historical Society, Denver, Colorado; pages 18, 36, 71, 74, 86, 98, and 106.

The Denver Public Library, Denver, Colorado; pages x, 9, 53, 66, 77, 78, 91, 102, 105, 109, 120, 121, 128, 153, 158, 172, and 175.

The Museum of New Mexico, Sante Fe, New Mexico; pages 6, 30, 44, 46, 58, 134, 138, and 143.

The Museum of the American Indian, New York, New York; pages 13, 61, 82, 83, 84, 85, 117, and 162.

The National Archives, Washington, D.C.; page 23.

The Southwest Museum, Los Angeles, California; page 141.

CONTENTS

MEDICINE MEN, HOT SPRINGS, AND DEATH

Early photo of a young Ute hunter with his bow and steel-tipped arrows and favorite dog. Photo by the Powell Survey.

INTRODUCTION

A few miles south of Cortez, Colorado, and northeast of Teec Nos Pos, the town of Towaoc rests on the side of a sagebrush-studded valley. Towards the south, an immense panorama of eroded buttes and sentinel rocks floats and fades mirage-like into the misty deserts of New Mexico and Arizona. This portion of the spectacular and timeless Four Corners region contains one of the three reservations still owned by the Ute Indian people.

A motorcycle engine starts with a noisy growl. Assorted pickup trucks driven by black-haired young men congregate in front of the Shell station. Some of the men, absorbed in quiet expressionless conversation, still wear shoulder-length hair, but none seem to wear braids in the old style. Up the street a cluster of new townhouses for the elderly is being completed midst a din of sawing and hammering. Beyond the new federal-government-sponsored housing, many older two- and three-bedroom bungalows now stand deserted; the clutter of old cars and grazing horses that once stood around them have been removed to new locations.

Silhouetted beyond the town of Towaoc is a wide, rolling valley colored with patches of blue-green desert grasses. An old Indian in faded Levis and a straw hat limps slowly across the rock-strewn prairie towards a group of multicolored horses. One by one they turn lazily to watch him approach. There are bays, sorrels, pintos, and a sand-colored palomino, all beginning to shed their heavy winter coats. They slowly gather at a barbed wire fence waiting to be inspected and petted and to muzzle against the old man's warmth as he tells them one of his stories about the old times. The old Ute's lined and leathery face tells much of the past, and when he dies, a little more of the tribal history will die with him.

The old people lived their history, felt it, and spoke of the past every day. It was too much a part of their personal life to record in some dusty archive, so they never bothered to develop a written language for the purpose beyond simple pictographs. Today, Ute tribal history slowly fades into the silent earth along with the older generation whose memories of the old ways no longer capture the imagination of the young.

"The whole valley is glowing and bright
and all the mountain peaks are gleaming
like silver" . . .

Fremont's Journals

WHO WERE THE UTES?

The Utes were called the "Blue Sky People" by other tribes. They were the feared and respected rulers of the "Shining Mountains." Their huge, rugged domain stretched from the eastern Front Range of the Rocky Mountains beyond Denver westward about 450 miles across the Continental Divide into central Utah, the state named for them. Ute lands extended from Shoshone country on the north along the Green River in Wyoming, southward across all of Colorado, and well into northern New Mexico. There was a time when Utes were commonly seen at Santa Fe. Their vast domain once covered about 150,000 square miles of beautiful mountain wilderness. These remote, part-woodland, part-plains, part-desert people were always considered different from their neighbors, the Sioux, the Cheyenne, and the Arapahoes. They are the only Indian tribe truly native to the state of Colorado. "Yuuttaa," they called themselves. Their dark-skinned ancestors roamed for untold centuries in semi-isolation amid America's most spectacular scenery. They were among the first North American tribes to acquire large numbers of "magic dogs" (horses) from the Spanish and were among the first accomplished Indian horsemen. Astride tough, sure-footed Spanish horses, their mobility, shrewdness, and subsequent fame grew swiftly, and soon Utes became feared and respected by their Indian neighbors for hundreds of miles surrounding the perimeters of their high-country domain. Yet for centuries they lived relatively isolated lives by choice in their pristine mountains far removed from most other tribes.

3

In 1776, a band of Utes befriended Father Dominguez and Father Escalante during their remarkable explorations in search of a new route to the Pacific Ocean through the canyons and desert lands of western Colorado and Utah. Ute hunters in the 1820s and 1830s aided and occasionally accompanied the early beaver trappers who were the first white men to penetrate the Rocky Mountains. Utes served as guides and became friendly with Jim Bridger, Uncle Dick Wootton, and Kit Carson, earning Colonel Carson's lifelong respect and, on most occasions, his friendship.

Ute shrewdness became better known as "Ute luck." By nature a shy people even by Indian standards, the Utes tended to avoid contact with the strange white people found probing around the fringes of their Rocky Mountain fortress. For two centuries they jealously and successfully resisted white incursions onto their lands. Intelligence and a fortunate geographic location allowed these rugged, individualistic people to live in freedom for 200 years, generally isolated from the overwhelming northward and westward migration of settlers going on around them. Not until the last quarter of the 19th century did the Utes lose their freedom to live as their ancestors had lived. The final containment came many decades after most North American Indian tribes had been locked up on poor, barren reservation lands and forced to attempt the painful assimilation process into the strange, white man's world.

On a warm September day in 1879, an insignificant, yet devastating incident, known variously as the Meeker Massacre and as the Thornburgh Battle, propelled the remote Colorado Ute tribe into headlines from Denver to Paris and Vienna. Before that bright fall day ended, Nathan Meeker lay dead among others, with a stake driven through his mouth.

Until that fateful day, the tribe managed through shrewdly negotiated treaties and a long list of clever delaying maneuvers to cling to a steadily dwindling, yet still vast and unspoiled homeland. Even by the late Victorian year of 1879, their undisputed territory included most of western Colorado, where they still hunted with the bow and arrow. That same memorable year, the first American patents were applied for involving the invention of an American gasoline motor car. Within a mere 25 years, the smelly machines would be chugging through Colorado country, and for most Coloradans, the ancient and durable Ute Indian people would be only a nostaglic memory.

Usually diplomatic, the Utes attempted to be cooperative with the greedy and aggressive trappers, gold seekers, and homesteaders, and were normally on friendly terms with the Spanish, Mexican, and United States military authorities. The final settlements between the Ute people and the federal government were negotiated in land, money, and supplies and eventually far surpassed the value of properties received by most tribes of similar size. Today, the Utes still retain title to three separate reservation lands, perhaps desolate in appearance to the casual observer but containing vast deposits of scarce energy resources.

Piah and other Utes with Winchester rifles. Photo by W.H. Jackson.

ANASAZIS TO "MAGIC DOGS"

The ancient origins of the Ute people lie shrouded in conjecture and educated guess. There may never be enough evidence found to provide continuity to their history. The Utes were first mentioned in Spanish territorial records kept at Santa Fe in 1626. At that time it was noted by a meticulous Spanish scribe that a mountain tribe of dark-skinned Indians known as Utahs had acquired a substantial number of Spanish horses. Governor Luis de Rosas, 1637-41, recorded the capture and punishment of approximately 80 "Uticahs," who were marched to a Spanish garrison and then turned to forced labor in the shops and industries at Santa Fe. It was more commonly recorded, however, that the "Utacas" frequently brought fine deerhides, buffalo robes, and captured Indian slaves to the Spanish outposts to trade for Spanish goods.

The early acquisition of horses by Ute traders and raiders quickly transformed the relatively backward tribe of food gatherers and hunters into a strong group able to resist successfully the incursions of their Indian neighbors and the attempted attacks by Spanish slave hunters. The Utes soon earned the respect of and a guarded friendship with the Spanish authorities at Santa Fe.

It is reasonable to assume that ancestors of the Utes were among those early Asian seekers of big game who successfully crossed the land bridge between Asia and Alaska and slowly wandered southward, following the animals and seeking the sun. It is also possible that predecessors of the Ute people were included among those gatherers and hunters who roamed about 10,000 years ago over wide areas of the southwestern United States and Northern Mexico, including west Texas, New Mexico, Arizona, Utah, Colorado, and parts of Wyoming.

Between the eighth and ninth centuries A.D., the great Mayan culture in Central America suddenly and mysteriously declined, sending refugees retreating from their homeland. Due to this period of unrest plus later infiltrating attacks by the Aztecs of Mexico, Mayan culture was undoubtedly felt outside its normal sphere of influence, including Mexico to the north. A later shock wave sent Aztecs of central Mexico fleeing in many directions to escape the cruel pressure and enslavement of the Christian forces invading from Spain. Undoubtedly, these movements had some reflected influence on the existing Indian tribes of the United States Southwest, as the desperate migrants from the south made contact with their neighbors through warfare, trade, and intermarriage.

The unique Ute language, which is so different from those spoken by Indian tribes from the eastern part of the North American continent, springs from a language group known as Uto-Aztecean. The language group is also referred to as Shoshonean and is a soft, pleasant-sounding, and melodious tongue. An ancient variation is still spoken by the Aztecs of central Mexico. Other Uto-Aztecean languages are spoken by the Comanches and Hopis, as well as the Pimas and Papagos of Arizona and the Piutes of Utah.

Enormous voids still remain in our understanding of the genetic and cultural backgrounds of the western Indian tribes. The first people positively known to have inhabited the Colorado plateau region are loosely referred to as the Folsom group. Very little physical evidence of these early people has been found. But one of their spear or atlatl javelin points has been discovered imbedded in the 10,000-year-old fossilized bones of a mammoth that once roamed the region. Remains of these huge furry elephants, along with those of camels and ancient bison, have been excavated from deposits located near Ft. Collins, Colorado, and elsewhere, and are now on display at Denver. Despite a dearth of discovered artifacts, it has been proven by pioneering paleontologists, such as Yale University's Othniel Marsh, that the Denver basin was extremely rich in animal life during large intervals of prehistory, and thus, would most likely have also been the home of ancient man.

The first well-documented evidence of man's permanent habitation in Colorado was found in the extreme southwest corner of the state, in the remote and arid canyon lands of the Four Corners region. There were many ancient settlements in this area. The many sites found at Mesa Verde are the most well known and the most accessible. These

Ute hunters scouting for game. The saddles and stirrups are U.S. military issue with Indian embellishment.

ruins were rediscovered through vague reports to local ranchers made by Indians living in the area. William Henry Jackson, the famed western photographer, traveled to a cliff house by mule in 1874 to record the first pictures. Five years later extensive amateur exploration was begun by the Wetherill brothers, local ranchers who discovered ruins of an entire cliff village while searching for lost cattle. Curiosity turned to profit when the Wetherills discovered that the artifacts they found in the ruined buildings could be sold for a good profit. As a result of this trade in antiquities, many valuable artifacts were lost before the ruins and their untouched remains could be protected by the creation of a national park authority at the site. Scores of ancient village sites have since been discovered in the Four Corners area, and discoveries of lesser importance continue to be made.

The earliest identifiable period of human occupancy at Mesa Verde has been designated as the Basket Maker culture and has been dated back about 2,000 years, to the time of Christ. Among the most recently discovered village sites is one located on the Ute Mountain Indian Reservation and another on the adjoining Southern Ute Reservation east of the tribal headquarters at Ignacio, Colorado. This isolated, windswept desert country has also revealed pithouses of the later Anasazi (Old People) culture. The ruins show that the Basket Makers had progressed by 500 A.D. to 750 A.D. into a thriving and an increasingly well-developed agricultural society. Some of the canyon-land groups possessed a sophisticated understanding of irrigation, and remains of their laboriously hand-dug canals show that water was diverted for many miles from rivers to support water-short crop lands. These people cultivated corn, beans, and squash, and in good years they traded their produce to more nomadic tribes in exchange for meat and hides. Occasionally the Mesa Verde villages were visited by Indian traders, who travelled vast distances from as far away as the Pacific Coast and the Mississippi River Valley. The discovery of artifacts made from shells found only in these far-flung locations attests to a brisk trade. The earliest bows and arrows, and pottery dating from the sixth century A.D., have also been discovered in the region.

Sometime before 1200 A.D. the Anasazi people, for reasons that we can only surmise, suddenly began to fortify their villages on the flat top of Mesa Verde. Then, about 1200 A.D., mysteriously and rather quickly, the old villages were vacated and the people moved into the precarious caves cut by wind and erosion into the sides of the cliffs just below the canyon rims. Here they built amazing apartmentlike structures complete with both round and square towers, showing such advanced knowledge of construction and masonry that a casual inspection makes it appear the structures were the work of the master builders who created medieval castles in western Europe at about the same time.

Suddenly after several generations, about 1276 A.D., both the caves and the mesas above them were strangely deserted, forever. No one is sure why the Anasazis left the security of their cliffside aerie or where they went. It is known that a severe 24-year drought hit the area about this same time. The time of the drought has been determined in part by tree-ring measurements that have recorded notably stunted growth during the period. Undoubtedly, the long, discouraging drought destroyed crop after crop. It may eventually have driven the game animals to less arid regions in search of food, causing a slow weakening of the people of the region and resulting in malnutrition and related sicknesses. A terrible time of famine may then have hastened the breakup and dispersal of the advanced Anasazi culture. Perhaps for several reasons, the people of the Four Corners region drifted off far away from their drought-stricken land. Many probably turned southward, to be assimilated into other tribes in central Arizona and New Mexico. Others may well have wandered north, following the game animals into the less dry, mountain high country of Colorado and Wyoming, or northwestward into the desolate desert lands of central Utah's Great Basin. Within this probable migration lies the thread of ancient Ute culture.

The Pah-Utes or Piute Indians roamed the dry Great Basin country of Utah until very recent times. Although related to the Utes, the Piutes are considered to be a separate and very different tribe. According to early Spanish, French, and American beaver trappers, the Piutes were notably backward people and were looked down upon by neighboring tribes. The Utes too, at one time, were considered poor by their Shoshone neighbors to the north. Reports from the early nineteenth century, including Captain (later General) Fremont's famous journals covering his western explorations, refer to the Piutes of Utah as leading a "mean, bare survival existence." The Piutes lived in crude pithouses, partially excavated into the desert floor and covered with brush, but they occasionally used wikiups, as did the Utes. These were hutlike structures made of brush and tree branches and sometimes plastered over with mud. The Piutes were stocky in build and unusually dark skinned. Some were reported as being only 4- to 4½-feet tall when they were first visited by white trappers. They wore very little clothing during the warm summers and were ill-clad for the cold winters in the Great Basin, and by the 1840s still did not own horses. Their sparse desert diet contributed to their being a weak, nonaggressive people. They existed on roots and berries, crickets, lizards, ants and grasshoppers, and various rodents and rabbits, and occasionally, planted a little corn and beans. On the positive side the Piutes were excellent basketmakers and left good petrographs and pictographs. They consider themselves cousins of the Utes.

Ute culture at the time of their first contact with the Spanish in the seventeenth century certainly showed similarities to Piute culture, both in habits and personal appearance. Ute families patiently trekked the meandering animal trails with their few possessions carried on the backs of squaws or on dog-powered travois. On foot they traveled east through the high mountain passes to Middle Park and Grand Lake, following the grazing buffalo herds eastwards and southward into South Park above Colorado Springs. Changes in life style occurred rapidly for the Utes after they acquired Spanish horses about 1640. On horseback they were able to cover far greater distances in a short time, penetrating the mountain passes of the front range on the eastern slope of the Colorado Rockies. Here they soon made contacts with the more advanced Plains Indians.

Through contact with advanced tribes and a greatly improved hunting ability facilitated by the use of the horse, these isolated Colorado mountain people finally emerged as a hardy, aggressive, and determinedly independent tribe. Very early, good horsemanship allowed the Utes to increase their trading with the Spanish and to mount successful raiding forays against the Plains tribes who roamed and hunted to the east of present-day Denver. Most of the more numerous Plains tribes were still on foot. The Utes admired their way of life as much as the Plains people admired and feared Ute horsemanship. Gradually the Utes began to adapt the Plains Indians' mode of dress. They discarded the leaky wikiup made of brush and mud in favor of the portable hide-covered teepees. it was the influence of Plains Indian society that slowly permeated and advanced Ute culture after 1640 and helped form the usually favorable portrait of them recorded by the early white trappers and explorers.

An unfortunate Spanish Soldier by the name of Alvar Nuñez, Cabeza de Vaca was the first explorer believed to have ventured into the

Ute sentry on a watchtower, circa 1900. Similar platforms were sometimes used for burials.

southwestern United States. Starting from Florida in 1528 after his expedition was shipwrecked, he began an incredibly difficult sea and overland journey, wandering westward along the swampy Gulf Coast and the Mississippi Delta country. Having lost his makeshift barges and completely losing his way, he and three other survivors spent several years of terrible hardship, sometimes enslaved among hostile Indian tribes. De Vaca, with a former black slave, Estivanico, finally emerged in Spanish Mexico where he had been considered dead and forgotten by his colleagues. De Vaca continued his trek westward through Mexico and possibly into southern New Mexico and Arizona for a journey that totalled eight years. Unfortunately, his strange exploits have been overshadowed by later expeditions.

Twelve years later, in 1540, Francisco Coronado set out from Mexico, with 250 mounted men in heavy cumbersome armor, up to 750 Indians, and a herd of cattle, on a well-publicized trip to explore northward beyond Mexico. Coronado's fame obliterates the fact that he was the second, not the first, European to visit the south central United States. His trips were guided in part by reports from de Vaca. Coronado hoped to prove the truth of the legends that were circulating throughout Spanish America regarding the existence of vast hordes of gold and silver in cities to the north. One legend told of the Seven Cities of Cibola, fabled cities of gold, reported to lie somewhere in the unexplored regions of northern New Mexico. Reports of the golden cities had been made by Estevanico, companion of Cabeza de Vaca. Vague stories of these cities had been told to him during his travels and long captivity among the Indians. Later, the stories were corroborated by Father Marcos de Niza, an overly exuberant and ambitious priest who, during a probing trip into New Mexico with friendly Indian guides, had in truth seen only a lonely Zuni pueblo on the far-distant horizon—shining golden in the sun.

There is no evidence that Coronado met Ute Indians. Yet such contact could easily have occurred, because Utes were known to be actively trading with Plains Indians at that time and with the Indian pueblos as far south of their mountain homeland as Taos and Pecos, New Mexico. Coronado is known to have visited an area close to eastern Ute territory. Word of his approach on "magic dogs," as the Indians labeled the wonderful horse, would certainly have spread to neighboring tribes and could have attracted many curious Indian spectators.

The first Spanish expeditions likely to have made contact with the Utes were those of Juan de Onate, who in 1608 attempted to locate Lake Copala (Great Salt Lake) in Utah. Although Onate did not penetrate much further than Abiquiu in northern New Mexico, it is likely that some of his men may have probed farther north. It became generally known at this time that Lake Copala was the land of the "Utaca" Indians.

Finally, in 1637, a scribe for Governor Luis de Rosas at Santa Fe, New Mexico, in the carefully written vellum record books of that day, described a battle between the governor's troops and a band of Utacas. This episode was the first historical mention of the Utes having acquired horses and was part of a punitive campaign against the surprisingly strong and elusive Utes from the north, undertaken to stop the widespread theft of Spanish horses and to halt Ute raids against the more docile Pueblo tribes. In this merciless battle, many Utes were killed and about 80 were captured, probably of the Maouche band that lived on the upper Rio Grande River. The Indians were driven to Santa Fe in chains, enslaved, and forced to labor in the workshops of the Spanish provincial capital. Undoubtedly many died early deaths because Indians were not used to intense labor.

During this period there were many Ute raids on outlying Spanish ranches to obtain horses, and in one successful attack in 1659, more than 300 horses were reported stolen and driven north into the mountains. At about the same time the Apaches, who were usually friendly and cooperative with the Utes, also began to acquire horses using the same hit-and-run raiding tactics.

Meanwhile, in far-off and troubled renaissance Europe, increasing numbers of migrants were leaving their homes to buy passage to the New World. The Inquisition, a powerful tribunal set up to investigate loyalty to the Roman Catholic Church in its struggle with disunity from within its own hierarchy, had reached its most ruthless and oppressive stage. Heretics, nonbelievers, and other suspected enemies of the church were imprisoned, tortured, or burned at the stake in increasing numbers. Religious and political tyranny reached such intensity in Spain that even loyal and affluent Spaniards fled to the New World to escape the wrath of the Church. The Inquisition greatly changed the history of Western Europe for centuries. It was initiated by Papal Bull in 1230 A.D. and was not officially terminated until well into the nineteenth century almost 600 years later. In addition, many thousands were also lured across the

Atlantic Ocean by reports of fabulous treasure to be plundered from the Indians of Mexico and Central and South America.

The early Spanish in the New World were accustomed to strict adherence to merciless religious codes of a demanding church and had little sympathy for the easy-going, nature-oriented customs of the Indians they encountered. Continuing the old practices of cruelty towards nonbelievers, the Spanish began to enslave and sometimes pointlessly slaughtered Indians of many tribes whom they found troublesome. Previously, and more disastrously, the Spanish had practiced near-genocide against the Incas, the Aztecs, and other tribes of Mexico and Central America. Since Indians were not Christian, they did not qualify for Christian charity and humane treatment. Forced labor, in chains, deep within gold and silver mines, proved too much for thousands of undisciplined tribesmen used to a leisurely outdoors life. The death rate was horrendous due to brutality, overwork, and frequent devastating epidemics of European diseases. The Indians had almost no natural resistance to such curses as smallpox and measles, which were imported along with the boatloads of invaders.

Soon the Indian labor force was so decimated that the Spanish authorities finally established reforms in order to keep their mining industry operating. It is estimated that as many as 15 million Indians died during the first 40 years of the Spanish conquest of America.

The Utes, being a nomadic people who lived far beyond the northern frontiers of Spanish power, were not easily subdued. It proved to be far simpler to control the non-migrating pueblo-dwelling tribes and even to deal with the fierce Navahos than it was to conquer the Utes. At the first sign of trouble the Utes would simply break camp and flee northward to the safety of their nearly impassable Rocky Mountains, taking borrowed Spanish horses with them.

Soon the Utes became well known among the Spanish settlements of northern New Mexico as being tough in battle and very shrewd at trading. They were one of the first tribes to earn the reluctant but pragmatic respect of the Spanish authorities at Santa Fe.

THE SEVEN BANDS

The Utes were pleasantly isolated in their Rocky Mountains by preference. During summer they followed the herds of deer and elk and buffalo on their annual migrations into the high timber and lush mountain meadows, rich with grasses and abundant varieties of berries and other plant foods. In winter, they followed the descending herds into the protected southerly river valleys to escape the cold winds.

The Utes had only occasional contact with the tribes that surrounded their mountain bastion. There were Shoshones in Wyoming to the north, where once their friends the Comanches had lived. Warlike Plains tribes lived to the east such as the Cheyennes, Arapahoes, Kiowas and the Sioux, and to the southeast lived the Comanches and Apaches. They followed the drifting herds of buffalo, as did the Utes. When hunting parties occasionally met, there was a shy, wary testing of each other's intentions, usually followed by trading and occasionally joint tribal dancing. Sometimes, if there was a disagreement over hunting grounds, a battle would result, depending upon the rivalries of the moment and the possible need for squaws by one of the groups.

Toward the southeast in southern Colorado and northern New Mexcio, the Utes had for centuries come into contact with the Jicarilla Apaches. They had traded, exchanged ideas, and occasionally intermarried to the point where the two tribes were usually allies and considered themselves distant cousins. Until 1748, the Utes were generally allied with the Comanches, too. The warlike Navajos and the advanced but sedentary Pueblo tribes of New Mexico were habitually raided by Ute war parties. In the western Utah desert plateau country lived the relatively poor and nomadic Piutes. They were true cousins of the stronger Utes. Limited intermarriage and an exchange of skills and hand-crafted goods had gone on for many centuries between the desert-dwelling Piutes and those who became Utes.

Ute with braided hair. Beaded neck bands were popular at the turn of the century. This one may have been store-bought or borrowed.

Generally the Utes were content to keep among themselves but were never afraid to fight an invading band of rival hunters in order to protect their privacy. They were nomadic loners more covetous of their independence than even their proud Indian neighbors on the plains.

A relatively small tribe, considering the vast area they controlled, the Utes were divided into seven fairly distinct bands or clans. Each band comprised friendly family groups, each of whom maintained a certain family independence, even within the band. Various groups rendez-voused once or twice a year, usually in winter, to trade, exchange news and stories, hold dances, and allow their sons and daughters to court. In time of war several bands might unite against the common enemy, usually a Plains tribe encroaching on their territory. Raiding expeditions were led by an elected war chief who could count on remaining the leader only so long as he held the respect of his men. Raids had the objective of protecting hunting territories, stealing enemy horses, kidnapping enemy women, or mounting a buffalo hunt inside enemy lands on the eastern Colorado plains.

Each Ute band had a carefully defined hunting territory, and it was dishonorable to hunt outside that territory without a bargaining powwow. Family groups within the band sometimes held a specific hunting territory that they had claimed for many years.

The seven generally recognized Ute bands were divided into four northern and three southern groups by the areas they traditionally occupied, although wintering and summering locations shifted over the centuries. The Mouache band of southern Utes lived in south central Colorado and northern New Mexico. They had very early contact with the Spanish near Taos and Santa Fe, along with the Capote Ute band who lived close by. These two bands in particular tended to intermarry with neighboring Apaches. The most well known Mouache leaders recorded by history include Mano Mocha, Delgadito, and Cuniache.

The Capote band was also southern Ute and lived in the rich San Luis Valley of southern Colorado and at the headwaters of the Rio Grande. Severo, Quiziachigiate, Buckskin Charlie, and Antonio Buck are known Capote leaders. The San Luis Valley, with its rich, well-watered potential farmland, drew the interest of hungry Spanish settlers at a very early date. There was periodic trouble with the tough Capotes, who generally managed to keep white settlers out of the valley.

The Weeminuche band of southern Utes occupied the San Juan River Valley and parts of northwestern New Mexico and southeastern

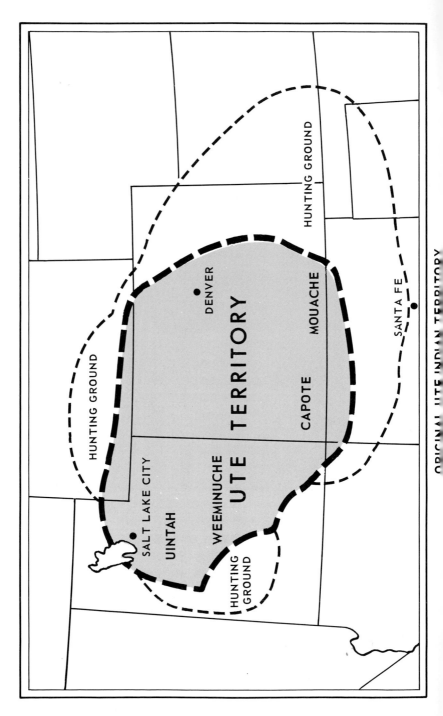

ORIGINAL UTE INDIAN TERRITORY

Utah. They were sometimes in contact with the less advanced Piutes, but they kept as far removed from the Spanish as possible. Their leaders included Cabeza Blanca and Ignacio. The Weeminuche comprise most of the present occupants of the Ute Mountain Reservation, which adjoins the Southern Ute Reservation.

The Tabeguache (or Uncompahgre) band lived along the deep, canyon-carved Gunnison River Valley and the valley of the Uncompahgre River in west central Colorado. They were considered a northern Ute band and were somewhat less exposed to the white man than the southern Capotes and Mouaches. The Tabeguaches were forced to follow the other northern Ute clans, including the ill-starred White River band and the Yampa or Colorado River band, to the Uintah Reservation during the dreaded forced march to Utah in 1880. The most successful and renowned of all the Ute chiefs, Ouray, was a Tabeguache, as was his popular predecessor, Nevava.

The Grand River band of northern Utes, also known as the Parianucs, usually lived along the banks and hills of the river now known as the Colorado, moving west to the lower valleys in the winter. The Yampa band of northern Utes inhabited the Yampa River Valley and the adjacent highlands, including the area of the present Routt National Forest. A splinter group of northern Utes came to be called the White River band for the region they occupied from the Colorado River north to the northwest corner of the state. They were an extremely shy and relatively unsophisticated group, many of whom steadfastly refused to accept the white man's authority. Their leaders were well reported during the Meeker incident and included Nicaagat (Captain Jack), Quinkent (Douglas), and Colorow.

The Uintah band of northern Utes lived south of the Great Salt Lake and occupied the Uintah River region of Utah east of Salt Lake City. They traditionally lived far removed from the other Ute bands and had very little contact with their fellow tribesmen. The Uintahs were a strong group who had been isolated from the mainstream of the tribe for hundreds of years, and although neighbors of the Piutes, there were distinct differences between the two groups. After the arrival of the Mormons under Brigham Young in the Salt Lake region, the Uintah Utes continued to live in relative peace with the settlers, thanks to a series of treaties signed by the Uintah leaders Souviette and Tabby. Although the Piutes lived in close proximity to the Uintah band, the latter were considered far more advanced. The Piutes did not acquire horses until very late in their history and led a generally backward life-style. In 1826 Jedediah Smith, an adventurous trapper, told of visiting a large village of Utes near the Great Salt Lake, and he commented on the notable differences between the Utes and the nearby Piutes.

There were noticeable differences between the various Ute bands too. Although opinions differ, it is generally accepted that the southern Ute groups progressed toward civilization faster during most of Ute history, probably due to their closer proximity to Spanish influence. As a negative consequence, they seem to have lost more of their cultural heritage and began to lose their cohesiveness as a tribe sooner. The Ute mountain band (Weeminuche) was considered very conservative; even though they were southern Utes, they became the last Ute group to set up their own government under the reservation system. The northern Utes, although generally less progressive, were fiercely independent. Their remote homeland kept them well insulated from foreign influences practically until the final removal to Utah in 1880. Although the Uintah group of northern Utes was backward during the early historical period, being more closely akin to the Piutes than to the other Ute bands, they progressed rapidly when given the stimulation of Mormon influence beginning in the mid-nineteenth century.

An interesting comparison has been drawn between the Uintah Utes of the Salt Lake region and the northern Ute bands from Colorado who were forced to live on the Uintah reservation after 1880. The study was made by anthropologist Dr. A. M. Smith. The Uintah Utes were found to be less sophisticated in their living habits than the White River Utes from northern Colorado. Among the comparisons made during study trips to various villages were the following:

	Uintah	White River Band
Sleeping blankets	Woven bark	Buffalo robes
Robes and coats	Rabbit skin	Bear & buffalo hide
Women's clothing	Partially nude in summer	Buckskin
Hair	Loose and unkept	Men in braids
Homes	Brush wikiup or crude teepee	Ornamented teepee

There is much speculation and very little information concerning the size of the Ute tribe before recorded historical contact with western

A Uainuint Paiute hunter aiming with rifle stand. Note the unbound hair typical of Paiutes of Utah. There is a probable kinship between the Utes and the Paiutes. Photo by John Hillers.

civilization. There is general agreement that no more than 5,000 to 10,000 Utes ever lived during a single period. Their number had apparently decreased due either to famine, war, disease, or intermarriage by the time Ute territory was visited by explorers and trappers in the 1820s to 1840s. At that time the Ute population was variously estimated to be between 3,500 and 4,000 people. The largest band to be observed was the Tabeguaches, estimated at about 1,500. No eyewitness account seems to have estimated the total Ute population at more than 4,500, a surprisingly small number of people to have dominated so vast a territory.

Ute influence on Colorado history and the history and development of the southwestern United States has been important and significant in spite of their limited numbers. Ute power and influence fully spanned the first 300 years of the white man's exploration and occupation of the continental United States. Yet, despite the fact that Ute territory included some of the best hunting grounds, richest mining territory, and most fertile valleys in the entire West, the Utes managed to keep out the aggressive Spanish settlers and soldiers for two centuries. No other Indian tribe ever seriously attempted to defy Ute power by occupying their huge Colorado mountain domain. Although hunting parties of Plains Indians occasionally ventured into Ute territory, there is no record of any invasion being launched against them with permanent settlement as its goal.

The Utes were feared by many neighboring tribes due to their recognized ability as defensive warriors. The difficult and rugged nature of their homeland gave them an advantage of maneuverability against invaders who were unfamiliar with their wild mountains. For centuries, the Utes were as possessively jealous of their well-stocked hunting territories as they were of their horses.

SPANISH RAIDS AND EXPLORING PADRES

In 1641 the new Spanish governor at Santa Fe decided to terminate an expensive and unsuccessful series of military actions against the Utes. The results of the campaign had been no better than a draw. Ute raids inflicted increasing damage to outlying Spanish ranchos and had terrified the people. Occasionally small Ute bands had been cornered and captured by Spanish troops, and on those occasions the Indians suffered punishing and cruel lessons in European warfare.

This first short but devastating war with the Spanish invaders seems to have deeply affected the Utes. Although never conquered or soundly defeated by the Spanish, they were impressed by the fact that they could never defeat the Spanish troops in pitched battle. Thereafter, showing exceptional shrewdness, the Utes accepted the hard fact of the white man's superior weapons and war-making ability and accepted peace with the Spanish governor. This peace settlement was unlike most treaties signed between the Indians and the white men because it spelled an end to general Ute hostility against the colonists. With only a few exceptions, the entire Ute nation managed to live in relative peace for the next 238 years with the steadily increasing tide of settlers living adjacent to their territory. Except for a notable period during the early eighteenth century, Ute warfare against the white immigrants became generally defensive rather than offensive.

The Utes continued to make occasional contact with gold prospectors, cattlemen, and farmers who probed the fringes of their lands attempting to push north from Spanish New Mexico, but contact was limited to occasional trading and was usually of short duration. Keeping to themselves in their remote Rocky Mountain meadows and river valleys, the Ute tribe posed very little threat to the westward- and northward-moving settlers and were little known to most Spanish and Yankee pioneers.

In 1670 the Spanish government of New Mexico signed the first formal treaty of peace between the Ute people and western civilization. The treaty was generally maintained by both sides. Trouble had been growing with several southwestern tribes, and the Spanish badly needed peace treaties to control an eroding stability.

In 1680 there was a fierce and widespread uprising of the Indians who lived in the New Mexican pueblo towns, under the leadership of the great Popé. His guidance proved to be exceptionally effective, and he managed, for a time, to unite not only the people of the pueblos, but neighboring tribes as well.

Driven by desperation brought on by generations of cruelty and exploitation by the Spanish, the allied tribes were finally successful in forcing the terrified European settlers and their garrisons of soldiers completely out of Taos, Santa Fe, and most of northern New Mexico. More than 400 Europeans were killed during the uprising by the vengeful Indians. Towns, ranches, and mission churches were burned in the intense and relentless guerrilla war, and the entire region reverted to Indian rule for a period of 10 years. Many irreplaceable Spanish records were lost or burned during the rebellion. The Utes, independent as always, never liked the Pueblo Indians and particularly despised the Navajos. During the uprising they refrained from taking sides and remained at peace with the Spanish.

As a result of the Pueblo Revolt, trade between the Utes and the Spanish was abruptly terminated. Each side feared treachery from the other due to wartime conditions, and few caravans ventured near Indian territory. Twelve years later, Spanish rule of the southwest had finally and ruthlessly been re-established by Diego de Vargas, and the old presidio at Santa Fe again dispensed European-style government. At about this time, during a trip north for meat and supplies, de Vargas met a band of Utes. He invited them to accompany him in peace back to Santa Fe, and after much hesitation, they finally accepted his offer. This friendly gesture opened a new period of Ute trading and contact with the Spanish settlements.

During the 1700s the Utes continued to increase the range of their territorial wanderings, and the strength and importance of their tribe grew. Trade with the settlements increased, and Utes became a familiar sight around the dusty presidios at Taos and Pecos and the little settle-

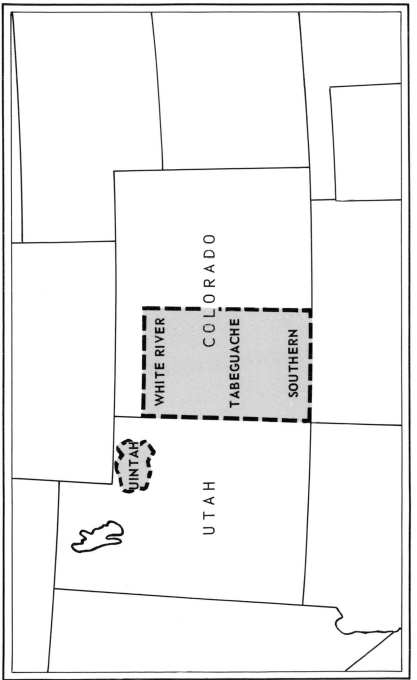

UTE INDIAN TERRITORY – TREATY OF 1868

27

ment of Picuris, and they occasionally continued to venture as far south as Santa Fe, the capital.

Ute raids on the Indians of the pueblos increased again, too. Often these raids were an unbalanced contest between well-mounted Ute warriors and an enemy settlement that had not been able to buy horses from the Spanish. There was also a short period of renewed raids by small Ute war parties against Spanish outposts, usually caused by some local dispute. It was obvious that the Utes were becoming a powerful tribe.

This was a period of confused tribal alliances and counter-alliances. As so often occurs when a tribal group or nation moves from a position of relative weakness to one of strength, alliances shifted quickly depending upon expedient advantage, and the Utes were not above exploiting their weaker neighbors.

Ironically, during this time the Jicarilla Apaches were sometimes at war with the Utes, even though they were considered distant cousins. The two tribes over the centuries have enjoyed long periods of friendship and intermarriage and have much in common regarding living habits and folklore. The Comanches, on the other hand, were Ute allies until 1748, at which time mutual grievances kindled 100 years of intermittent war between the two Uto-Aztecean speaking neighbors. An attempt at a peace treaty between the two tribes was made about 1870, when a great powwow was held between the Utes, led by Buckskin Charlie, chief of the southern Utes, and the Comanches, led by the powerful Quanah Parker. After lengthy ceremonies, the treaty was about to be formalized when an unknown Indian in the encampment fired a rifle shot. This was enough to terminate the peaceful powwow for the next 100 years. Finally, in 1977, after more than 200 years in a state of war, the two tribes signed a peace treaty at Ignacio, Colorado.

Not until 1719 was the long period of peaceful relations between the colonial government at Santa Fe and the tribe seriously threatened. In that year small bands of both Utes and Comanches were accused of making raids against Spanish ranches. They were unsuccessfully pursued by Spanish colonial troops northward, only to disappear into rugged mountain passes. Later, in 1746, fresh troops were brought from Mexico and ordered against the Indians by Governor Joachim Coadallos y Rabel. This time, rather than returning to their safe mountain retreat to the north, the Utes agreed to join the Comanches in a common defense. Near Abiquiu, New Mexico, the combined Indian force tried to repeat an earlier victory over the Spanish by the Navajos, but in this case the Indian army was soundly defeated. In 1750, tired of frequent skirmishing, the Utes again made an expedient peace with the Spanish. Partially because of the unsuccessful Ute-Comanche alliance and the willingness of the Utes to make a separate treaty with the Spanish, a long war between the Utes and the Comanches began.

The 1750 treaty with the rulers of the Colorado mountains again gave the Spanish an opportunity to increase their trading and fur trapping northward, close to Ute territory. By the 1760s, there were frequent Spanish expeditions heading into southern Colorado to trap and trade for furs and skins, which were increasingly in demand in Europe. These hunting expeditions were sometimes joined by independent commercial traders who rode north in a carreta, a bulky cart with two huge solid wooden wheels, often pulled by lumbering oxen. The traders bartered glass beads, mirrors, flour, blankets, and sometimes guns for finest quality Ute deerskin and buffalo hides. For many years it had been illegal under Spanish law to sell horses to the Indians, but by this time the Utes were successfully breeding their own stock and were no longer dependent upon Spanish horses.

On one expedition Juan de Rivera and his party penetrated as far north into Colorado as the junction of the Gunnison and Uncompahgre Rivers near present Delta, Colorado. Rivera was hunting for fur pelts and was also looking for gold, which had been rumored to occur in the mountains. Rivera did locate traces of silver ore, but returned home without having made significant discoveries. On his travels he passed the later sites of the towns of Ignacio and Mancos on the Dolores River. Very little record remains of these first Spanish probing expeditions into Colorado and Ute territory.

During the spring of 1776, a Declaration of Independence for the American colonies was being hotly debated by the Continental Congress at Philadelphia. Meanwhile, 1,500 miles to the west, at Santa Fe, two enthusiastic priests were making last-minute preparations for a long, dangerous trip. Father Francisco Dominguez had recently received new orders from Mexico City regarding the managing and inspection of Indian missions in the Southwest. Included with these orders was another rather vague assignment made almost as an afterthought by his superiors. The priest was authorized to investigate the possibility of locating a shorter overland route between the northern New Mexican settlements and the prosperous chain of Spanish missions in California recently established by Father Junipero Serra. Spanish interests on the

Don Diego de Vargas, Marquis, Captain General and Governor of New Mexico, subdued the Indians following the 10-year pueblo rebellion and made peace with the Utes.

west coast were growing rapidly and a new road westward was badly needed. The proposed route lay through rugged, uncharted country, lands known to be inhabited by the wild "Yutas."

Father Dominguez selected as his assistant on the trip a young 25-year-old priest from Spain, Silvestre Velez de Escalante. The mission priest at the Zuni Pueblo, he was also an astute reporter and already had visited the Hopis to the west of his mission. The expedition was routed towards the northwest in order to avoid a huge, impassable canyon (the Grand Canyon) and Indian tribes there that were reported to be cannibalistic.

At first the expedition was not granted sufficient financial support to equip for a long trip, but at the last moment the Spanish governor reluctantly supplied additional funds. As a condition for approving and supplying the expedition, the governor required that attempts be made to locate gold deposits and evidence of gold stored among the Indian tribes met along the way. Retired Captain Don Bernardo Miera y Pacheco agreed to accompany the expedition as military adviser and cartographer.

Early on the morning of July 29, 1776, 10 days after the American Declaration of Independence was formally read to the people on Boston Common, the Dominguez-Escalante expedition, a little band of Spanish soldiers, civilians, Indian guides, and two enthusiastic priests, left Santa Fe, New Mexico. They headed northwest on the first well-documented trip through the heart of the immense, uncharted, Ute Indian territory.

The 12 adventurers first traveled down the Dolores River close to the western border of Colorado. In the vicinity of present Montrose, Colorado, the expedition met the first "Yuta" Indian traveling with his family. Andres Munoz, a Pueblo Indian guide accompanying the expedition, spoke fluent Ute and persuaded the Ute family to join the Spanish party. The shy "Yuta" introduced himself as "the Left Handed." He was given gifts of a knife and beads and a warm wool blanket. In exchange, he agreed to guide the expedition northwest through Ute territory towards central Utah. But instead, "Left Handed" persuaded the party to first turn northeastward to visit his people, the Sabagana Yutas (Tabeguaches), then at their summer hunting encampment on top of Grand Mesa.

The party followed a relatively easy route up the North Fork of the Gunnison River past present Paonia to Hubbard Creek. Taking a rocky canyon trail up to the mesa top, they entered one of the Utes' favorite and most beautiful hunting territories, a region of lush forests and lakes teeming with game. The Ute encampment of teepees on Grand Mesa held about 100 people, and the padres were welcomed warmly. Although the Utes knew vaguely of the Spanish settlements far to the south, only a few had ever seen a white person.

After distributing gifts, Father Dominguez held the curious Indians spellbound with hours of fervent Christian preaching. Through Munoz, his Spanish Indian interpreter, he attempted to explain to the "heathen" Utes about the great, all-encompassing power of the white man's God. As always, the Indians were courteous and listened to the strange man dressed in his unusual priest's cassock. At least the large cross he carried was somewhat familiar to the Utes. The crossed-pole symbol was similar to a design commonly used by many Indian tribes in pictographs, bead-work, and blankets. After more gifts were exchanged, the Utes politely agreed to accept the priest's message about Christianity. At least it was so reported in the daily journal kept by Father Velez de Escalante. Accep-tance of the faith lent a certain technical protection to the Indians by the church and of course enhanced the importance of the expedition.

Ute tradition of hospitality demanded that the padres visit inside the Ute teepees to smoke a pipe and eat. The squaws had been busily preparing food for the expected feast since the arrival of the expedition. Finally, after some hesitation, the wary priests agreed to enter the teepees and unenthusiastically forced down strange Indian food. While smoking pipes, the Ute elders warned the Spaniards about the dangerous Shoshones who lived to the north and told stories about cannibalistic in-dians that might be encountered if the expedition continued toward the northwest. The Utes argued that the priests and their followers should immediately return to Santa Fe for their own safety.

Not to be intimidated, the padres were finally able to trade their tired horses for fresh Ute mounts and continued on their way north. "Left Handed," the Ute guide who had been christened Anastasio by Father Dominguez, agreed only to lead the party a short distance across the Grand River (Colorado River) to the mouth of the White River. Fear-ing enemy tribes, he refused to go further. There the Ute guide left the little party with a friendly Laguna Indian who had been visiting the Ute encampment on Grand Mesa. The new Laguna guide was named Silvestre by the party, and he led them on the long trek to the villages on the shore of Utah Lake (the Great Salt Lake).

The expedition had left Santa Fe too late in the summer season for so long a trip. Unknown to the intrepid travelers, 800 miles still lay between them and the Pacific Coast, and it was now late September. Some felt Monterey on the central California coast could not be more than a week's travel away, but Captain Miera y Pacheco felt differently. From earlier sketchy reports received from wandering Indian traders, he accurately calculated that the trip would take much longer and winter was fast approaching. In effect, the Dominguez-Escalante party was lost in the high plains and valleys of northern Utah. So, after preaching to the Indians they found living in the great valley near the Salt Lake shore, the party reluctantly turned south.

The expedition had accomplished a major feat by reaching the formerly mythical lake and had explored a vast new territory, but they were not to accomplish their mission to map a new route to the Pacific. Disappointed and dangerously low on supplies, they now searched for a safe trail through the rugged, dry canyon country of Utah back to Santa Fe. Their return trip was filled with hardship as they meandered down the cliffs and through the unhospitable desert country of southern Utah and the parched high plains of northern Arizona. Some of the horses had to be eaten when there was no more game to be hunted. One cold night, Captain Miera y Pacheco became ill and seemed near death. It was not until January 2, 1777, that the bedraggled, half-starved little group appeared again in the dusty central plaza at Santa Fe.

The Dominguez-Escalante expedition was considered a failure. It had wasted church funds without realizing its objective. As a result, Father Dominguez was demoted in the church hierarchy, charged with failure to map a new route to the California missions and for neglecting his other administrative duties.

In truth, the 1,500-mile trip into unmapped Colorado and Utah was a tremendous breakthrough. It charted the vast Ute domain in fair detail, and Father Escalante's careful journals gave a vivid description of the wild, spectacular country. The expedition's records proved of great benefit to the later mapping of new routes to California.

A tradition of friendship between the Ute people and the Spanish settlers continued for a time. Trade grew. Typically, Spanish traders from Abiquiu, Taos, and Santa Fe traveled north fairly regularly with their ox carts into the fringes of Ute country in Colorado, and may have penetrated as far as the Gunnison River. The Utes began to prepare and cure more fine-quality deerskin and buffalo hides especially for the Spanish trade. Ute deerhide and soft, supple doeskin was considered of the best quality and was much in demand by Spanish ladies. Increased trade brought the Utes iron household utensils, knives, beads, small hand mirrors, guns, and warm Spanish wool blankets much admired by the Indians for their light weight.

Very early, and quickly, the Utes had learned the fine points of horse breeding and veterinarian skills from Spanish ranchers, and they became widely recognized as expert horse breeders. Their own herds had been steadlily expanded, and they were soon in a position to enter into lucrative horse trading.

Tough, smallish Spanish "Barb" horses were originally bred in North Africa by the Moors as early as the eighth century and were introduced into Spain during the Moorish conquests. Brought to the new world by the Spanish, this breed was crossbred by the Utes and other tribes with stolen and stray horses of many different breeds. In later times wild horses that were descendants of various other breeds brought over by early expeditions to the New World could be caught and crossbred as well. One product of the crossbreeding was called Pinto, a tough, smallish horse of about 14 hands, ideally suited for travel in the rugged mountain country. The tall, waving Colorado grasses found in the river valleys and high meadows were extremly rich in minerals, and Ute horses grew strong and thrived on the good care provided by Indian owners. Fine horses became the greatest wealth and pride of the Ute nation, and an especially prosperous Indian family might own several hundred.

In 1779, the Comanches, who like most Indian tribes hated the Spanish for their cruelty and exploitation, had increased their raiding and killing among the outposts in New Mexico. Governor Juan Batista de Anza, after lengthy negotiations, enlisted the assistance of the friendly Mouache Ute band and the Jicarilla Apaches in a campaign to punish the Comanches. The Comanches were a branch of the Shoshone tribe, who had ancient ties with the Utes themselves. By offering their Ute Indian allies the spoils of battle when the hated Comanches were defeated, plus the gift of new guns and horses, the governor's royal troops were joined by 200 Utes and Apaches. The combined army pursued the Comanches, who were led by the able Chief Greenhorn, through northern New Mexico into Colorado. After many days of fruitless tracking the Spanish and Indian force of over 1,000 men finally was able to corner Greenhorn's band on the upper Arkansas River at Greenhorn Creek near present Walsenburg. In a vicious battle, the Comanches were badly defeated, and the survivors scattered through the countryside. Their famous war chief was killed during the fighting, and much booty was taken by the Utes. Many Comanche slaves were taken back to Santa Fe in chains.

This successful campaign was followed by a second formal treaty of peace between the Mouache Utes and the Spanish. It was agreed to in 1789, and for the signing, the Utes accepted gifts. The alliance helped the Spanish by taking pressure off their troops, who were almost constantly needed to patrol and guard outlying settlements and the docile, subjugated Pueblo villages against raids by the Navajos and other angry tribes. The controlled Pueblo villages were very important to the Spanish and were administered more or less as labor factories to turn out workers for the settlements.

The Comanches sought revenge against the Utes for the killing of Chief Greenhorn on the Arkansas River, and their chance for retribution finally came in 1809. In that year in the same Arkansas River basin, 600 Mouache Utes and Jicarilla Apaches were attacked by a combined force of Comanches, Kiowas, and Cuampes. In the terrible ensuing battle, no less than three important Mouache leaders were killed—Mano Mocha, El Albo, and most important, Chief Delgadito. This was a crushing blow to Ute pride and prolonged the long period of animosity between the Utes and Comanches.

Lt. Zebulon M. Pike led the first American expedition through Ute territory while exploring the Louisiana Purchase. He was scouted by Utes, leading to his capture by the Spanish. He died a general at age 34 during the War of 1812.

YANKEE TROOPS AND BEAVER TRAPPERS

Zebulon Pike was a very young man when he left his name firmly established in American history. In fact, his name has become more renowned due to the mountain named after him than the results of his early exploratory trip might indicate. Pike was a United States Army lieutenant when he became identified with Colorado, and was destined to die a brigadier general and a hero during the War of 1812 at the age of 33. He was the first U.S. citizen known to have entered Colorado territory from the east and to have approached the foothills of the Rocky Mountains. He is also probably the first American citizen to have been guided by the Ute Indians. In 1806, the United States purchase of the Louisiana territory was only three years old, and it included part of what is now Colorado. The purchase arranged by Napoleon to finance his military campaigns had been called "folly" by the American ex-minister to France and financier Gouverneur Morris. Lieutenant Pike, by presidential order, was sent to explore the headwaters of the far-off Arkansas and Red Rivers, which were considered to be the southern boundary of the Louisiana Purchase.

In the summer of 1806, Pike traveled west with a small command of 23 men to within sight of the soaring Rockies. Wisely, he did not attempt to cross these seemingly impassable peaks. Unwisely, he turned south, marching his small band onwards toward hostile territory. The actual boundaries of the Louisiana Purchase were very much in doubt, and the borders had been contested by Spain. During the march south beneath the Front Range of the Rockies, Pike was accompanied by paid Ute Indian guides. Unknown to Pike, the Spanish territorial governor at Santa Fe, His Excellency Joachim Allencaster, had been notified of the approach of a United States military force by couriers. He asked Mano

Mocha, the powerful Mouache Ute war chief, to scout the approaching party and report the location and activities of the United States soldiers. When Mano Mocha's runners reported that Pike had entered the San Luis Valley in southern Colorado, the Spanish sent a force of 100 men to try to intercept the Americans.

It was by then December, and Pike's small group of soldier explorers and cartographers was running very low on supplies. He was camped hundreds of miles from the nearest supply base, and his situation was becoming desperate. Finally, on Christmas Day, his hunters located and shot eight buffalo, saving the party from starvation. Experiencing early winter snowstorms and strong gales, the party rested in uncomfortable quarters until early January and then, during a brief period of milder weather, continued south past great sand dunes, now the Sand Dunes National Monument. Not far from the dunes, on the Conejos River, the American party was intercepted by the stronger force of Spanish troops. Despite Pike's insistence that he was simply lost and not intending to invade Spanish territory, he was arrested and transported to Santa Fe, where he became an unwilling guest of the governor. After polite interrogation and some entertainment by the people of the town, Lieutenant Pike and his men were sent south to temporary confinement at Chihuahua, Mexico. Pike finally reached New Orleans after four months in a Mexican jail. The report of the Pike expedition was published back East and excited widespread speculation about the southwest and about the rich trade possible at booming Santa Fe.

Lieutenant Pike, in his journal, reports several incidents involving the Ute tribe. He comments about a battle between the Utes and Pawnees in which well-mounted Utes were pitted against unmounted Pawnee foot soldiers. He also tells of a battle reportedly held at Taos between the Utes and the Comanches, during which eight to ten Indians were killed on each side. The battle was finally stopped by the Spanish *alcade* of the town, who bravely rode his horse between the opposing groups of some 400 Indians and pursuaded them to disperse.

After 200 years of complete Spanish dominance of the American Southwest, the Louisiana Purchase finally cracked open the door to Spain's jealously guarded western empire. The expanding United States government sent numerous mapping and exploratory expeditions into the immense new territory. Trappers and mining men quickly began to probe the possibilities of the new-found American West.

In 1820, Major Stephen Long explored along the Front Range of the Colorado Rockies and passed the present sites of Denver and Colorado Springs. A botanist traveling with his party reported seeing a well-worn Indian trail leading into the mountains. This was Ute Pass, now a paved, partially four-lane highway running from the Manitou Springs into South Park.

After 1823, the independent Mexican government, recently freed from Spanish control by revolution, tried to continue peaceful relations with the Utes. As a result of good relations, Mexican wagon trains loaded with trade goods were allowed to travel westward from Santa Fe unmolested, on a trail to Los Angeles along the southern edge of territory inhabited by the Capote Ute band. Inevitably, settlers eager to reach California began to follow the wagon trains in large numbers. Others searching for good land tried to settle in the fertile valleys near the southern borders of Colorado where several early Spanish land grants had been established but never successfully colonized. These new farms and ranches were repeatedly attacked by both the Utes and the Navajos, and as a result of constant harassment, the influx of Mexican immigrants was successfully checked for the time being.

In Europe, where the population was rapidly increasing, the important supply of fur for coats and hats had steadily dwindled. Luxurious fur from far-off North America was in great demand by an increasingly affluent population. The forests east of the Mississippi, once filled with game, were already depleted. News about the vast hunting grounds of the Louisiana Purchase created great excitement and a rush to control the new fur trade in this vast midsection of the American continent. As early as 1812, Ezekial Williams was reported to have trapped for fur in Ute territory in southwestern Colorado. He was followed shortly by Robert McKnight and by the intrepid French trappers Chouteau and De Munn. In 1821, small, adventurous groups were led into Ute territory by Colonel Glenn and by Jacob Fowler. Encounters between the Utes and these early parties of exploring hunters were generally friendly, because there was plenty of game for everyone. Some of the early trappers undoubtedly hunted through Ute territory without seeing any Indians at all, because the tribe was not large and was thinly spread over the vast Colorados wilderness.

Strangely, a new style in men's headgear in far-off Europe was soon to cause the Utes and other western tribes increasing aggravation and competition for their hunting grounds. New, tall hats covered with luxuriant dark chestnut, beaver fur were suddenly the rage of London and Paris, and every well-dressed gentleman coveted one. The supply of beaver in Europe and sources subsequently exploited in the eastern United States were soon exhausted. Not so along the beautiful meandering river bottoms throughout the Rocky Mountain region and the high western plains. Ironically, the beaver hat was partially responsible for forcing the shy, independent Utes to meet and cope with the increasing number of Europeans and Americans entering their private world.

Whereas the Spanish had very little reason to venture into Ute territory, American, British, French, and Mexican fur trappers by the hundreds now began to pour into Colorado, Wyoming, the Dakotas, and even into Utah and Nevada. During the 1820s and 30s trading posts, and forts to protect them, were established around the fringes of Ute territory. For many years, the Hudson Bay Company enlisted contract hunters and trappers to supply the growing fur trade. Moving westward and south they sent their hunters throughout the Rocky Mountain region. Often advance payments were made to the trappers for supplies, because a successful beaver-trapping trip might take four to six months to complete. Soon John Jacob Astor's new American Fur Company began to give the British Hudson Bay Company stiff competition by hiring the best hunters and offering better prices for their furs.

The Utes and other tribes found beaver trapping profitable too. White trappers began to visit the Ute encampments to buy furs and sometimes simply to socialize in the big, lonely country. Bill Williams and the almost-legendary Uncle Dick Wootton were famous among trappers of the period and became friendly with the Utes. Dick Wootton was probably the first United States citizen to negotiate his own private treaty with the Utes. He was given personal safe passage through western Colorado on his trapping expeditions. Bill Williams lived and hunted with his Ute friends periodically and became a familiar figure in the Ute villages telling stories around their campfires. Unfortunately, one day while traveling alone through Ute territory, "Old Bill" was not recognized by a roving Ute war party and was shot and killed by mistake.

In 1834, Jim Bridger, Isaac Rose, and a young runaway apprentice from Missouri named Christopher "Kit" Carson made contact with the Utes. Kit Carson had recently signed up as a fur trader for John Jacob Astor's American Fur Company, and he and his party hired Ute guides to lead them on a trapping expedition to the Humboldt River in Utah, where beaver had been reported in great quantities, a report that turned out to be erroneous. On this trip Isaac Rose later recalled having borrowed bows and arrows from the Indians to learn their method of killing grizzly bears. After sending many arrows in the direction of an unfortunate beast without apparent effect, a Ute hunter finally had to finish the job. Riding wildly past the bear on his horse, the Indian cooly dispatched the animal with a single arrow through the lung.

Each July or August during the height of the beaver trade, great fur-trading fairs were held. Summer is the season when beaver lose their beautiful coats and, therefore, cannot be trapped. So, at this time of year, the wildest and most popular meetings were held deep in the wilderness along the Green River in Wyoming, in territory claimed by the Wind River Shoshones, but occasionally visited by Ute hunting parties. The Utes hunted in southern Wyoming west of the continental divide when the buffalo and elk herds led them there, but the Shoshones did not like these incursions into their coveted hunting lands. Small groups of Utes and visitors from many tribes were drawn to the summer trapper get-togethers to trade their furs and skins. The fairs were rowdy, carousing events attended by lonely trappers with plenty of money to spend and no way to spend it. Large quantities of whiskey were packed in by enterprising merchants, but very few women could ever be persuaded to attend. There was wild, enthusiastic dancing, and if female partners were unavailable, the rough trappers danced with each other. Itinerate evangelical preachers, as well as the renowned Reverend Marcus Whitman and Dr. Parker, who visited the fair one summer while enroute to Oregon, held tent revivals trying to save souls. They were reported to have been well attended, and the collection plates were easily filled. Preaching amused the Indians who came in from the hills with their squaws to watch the strange raucus activities. The Indians had beaver pelts to sell and sometimes brought captured women from enemy tribes, who were traded to to the lonely trappers for knives, blankets, flour, and whiskey and guns. Pelts brought by the Indians usually brought lower prices than prices demanded by the white trappers due to discrimination on the part of the fur buyers. Unfortunately, the great trading fairs did not survive for many years and soon died out with the decline of the beaver trade.

In 1826, James "Ohio" Pattie passed the present site of Grand Junction, Colorado on the largely unexplored western slope of the Rockies.

The Utes, after lengthy negotiations, reluctantly allowed the indominable trapper Antoine Robideaux to open a small trading post four miles below the junction of the Uncompahgre and Gunnison Rivers.

Unfortunately, the romantic fur trading era was to be short-lived, and by 1840, it was already drawing to a close. Fine silk from China was replacing beaver as a covering for men's tall hats. Improved woolen production in Europe and America was keeping the public warmer and was decreasing the need for furs. Also, in 1840 the Utes became tired of intrusion by the trappers and decided to burn down Antoine Robideaux's trading post. But the pushing and probing of Americans into the Rocky Mountain West had just begun. Mexicans also were pressing and shoving from the south. For many years the Spanish had attempted to establish ranches in southern Colorado on the early land grants made by the king, but had always been driven out by the Indians. A stalwart group of Mexicans again tried to establish a farming settlement at Antonito in 1843. After some delay, a Ute council was held to decide what should be done about this new intrusion. The elders feared war with the Mexicans might result if the settlement were attacked, but younger leaders argued that there was a greater danger to the tribe if settlements were allowed to gain a foothold in the San Luis Valley. Finally, the younger warriors prevailed, the new settlement was burned to the ground, and the Mexican settlers were again driven out of Ute territory. The first permanent Mexican settlement in Colorado, San Luis, was not established until 1851, eight years later, and it became the first permanent nonmilitary town to be established in the state.

Unknown to the Utes, the Treaty of Guadelupe-Hidalgo, which ended the Mexican War of 1846-48, ceded all of New Mexico and southern Colorado to the United States. In its provisions, the United States agreed to honor certain old Spanish and Mexican land grants, including some located inside Ute territory. Like the Spanish before them, the new U.S. military government soon recognized the strength and independence of the Ute people. Losing no time, they persuaded the Utes to meet for a conference at the old Spanish outpost of Abiquiu north of Española in New Mexico.

The ancient adobe village of Abiquiu with its mission church and typical town plaza had long been a Spanish military garrison post and a collecting point for Indian slaves and captives. The town overlooked the rich river-bottom farmland of the Rio Chama. Because of its closeness to

Indian territory, many important conferences and treaty negotiations with various tribes were held here by the Spanish, Mexicans, and later by the Americans throughout the colonial period and settlement of the Southwest.

The Utes were represented at the Abiquiu conference with the Americans by 28 elders, mainly from the Capote and Moauche bands, and by Chief Quiziachigiate, a Capote. A formal treaty was drawn and signed and was later endorsed by Chief Nevava and other Tabeguache Ute leaders, including Salvadore. Although not truly a chief himself, Salvadore was the father of Ouray, greatest of the Ute chiefs. It was December, 1849, and this historic treaty conference was the first to be held between the Ute nation and the new American government in the West. Gifts were distributed by the American representatives, and a payment of $5,000, per year was promised to the Utes. In exchange, the Utes agreed to accept the terms of the Treaty of Guadalupe-Hidalgo and to acknowledge authority of the United States government in the area. There were no territorial boundaries estalished for Indian lands.

The next year an Indian agency was opened by the United States government at Taos, New Mexico, to deal with the Capote and Moauche Utes and also to serve the Pueblo people of the area. Kit Carson became the Indian agent at Taos in 1853 and held the post for six years. Kit Carson, called "Rope Thrower," was very popular among the Indians. He had known the Utes previously during his eight years as a young beaver trapper in Colorado and had won their lasting friendship. The Utes were very disappointed when their friend Rope Thrower married Looking Glass, a pretty Arapahoe girl, because her people had been bitter rivals of the Utes for centuries. Carson was a rough and largely illiterate man, but intelligent and very ambitious. He had run away from his Missouri home as a teenager, where he had been unhappily apprenticed to a saddlemaker. Later, after extensively travelling the Rocky Mountains as a trapper, he became a guide for Captain John C. Fremont and, with Fremont and General Kearny, rendered brilliant military service during the "liberation" of California. Still later, Carson's second wife, a Spanish girl from a good family in Santa Fe, taught him to read and write. In 1863, as colonel and subsequently brigadier general of the 1st New Mexico Volunteers, Carson led 1,000 men, including a group of Ute scouts, on a climactic campaign to punish the Navajos who had been raiding the newly established homesteads in the territory. After a cam-

Abiquiu, New Mexico: the central plaza, 1915-20. This was an early northern outpost of Spanish New Mexico. Many Indian negotiations occurred here.

paign of scorched earth during which Navajo villages and their prized peach orchards were burned, Carson forced the battered Indians into a concentration camp at Bosque Redondo, New Mexico. His brutal tactics brought the Navajos under control, but it destroyed much of the trust and respect he had formerly enjoyed from the Indians of the region. Later, however, Carson was able to renew his friendship with the Utes due partially to their ancient dislike of the Navajos. He took part in the successful treaty negotiations with Ute leaders in Washington, D.C., in 1868. On the way home from this trip Carson died.

A seldom-remembered incident in Kit Carson's life involved the Utes, and was perhaps the most embarrassing moment in his career. During the period when David Meriwether was commandant at the newly acquired American outpost at Abiquiu, the Utes sometimes camped opposite the town on the Chama River to trade. One day, Meriwether ordered Kit Carson to visit the Ute camp to continue certain ongoing negotiations. Hearing noise and seeing general confusion in the Ute encampment, Carson learned that the band was preparing for battle with a group of Navajos said to be approaching the area.

Fearing trouble, Carson refused to leave Abiquiu to visit the Indians across the river. Commandant Meriwether became infuriated with Carson for refusing to obey his order and had him thrown in jail. To the consternation of Carson's later admirers, the popular folk hero was formally charged with cowardice and insubordination and spent two days in confinement. The facts of the case generally support Carson's actions during the episode.

Christopher "Kit" Carson in his uniform as Colonel of the First New Mexico Volunteer Infantry.

"A GRAND BED OF SNOWCAPPED MOUNTAINS ROSE BEFORE US"—

Fremont's Journals

At the same time that American authority was being established south of Ute territory in New Mexico, a smaller, peaceful invasion was taking place to the north in the Rocky Mountains. John C. Fremont, still in the early chapters of his long, eventful career and now an army topographical engineer, made trips into the western territories, including three successful exploratory and mapping tours through much of the Rocky Mountain region.

On the second trip, Fremont's party covered the Colorado high country, mapping mountains and rivers and canyons in considerable detail. His party traveled from Wyoming southward through Middle Park, passing the present sites of Kremmling and Breckenridge, and continued southeast to present Pueblo, Colorado. Fremont's most publicized trip took his party of 60, including Creoles, French, French Canadians, and Americans, up the Arkansas River, over Tennessee Pass, and down the western slope of the Rockies. He then journeyed on to California, where he eventually joined Colonel (later General) Stephen Kearny. Fremont helped to gather a military force strong enough to attack the Mexican garrisons stationed along the California coast, and in a successful campaign, all of California was wrested from Mexican rule.

Luck followed both Fremont and the California territory. In 1850, one year after the first gold strikes on the American River, John Fremont struck it rich himself. His men discovered valuable gold deposits on his vast California estate. Fremont's wife, who was the daughter of powerful Senator Thomas Hart Benton of Missouri and a talented writer, helped edit her husband's reports of his western expeditions. The sensational Fremont report was published by the government and became an instant success in the East, receiving wide press coverage. His journals helped to encourage and guide thousands of eager migrants and gold seekers through the Rocky Mountains to the Pacific coast.

Fremont's journals were published as a *Report of the Exploring Expeditions to the Rocky Mountains* by Brevet Captain John C. Fremont, 1843-44. They contain some fascinating early accounts of the Colorado country and of the Utes. Fremont followed the Platte River, which he called the Nebraska River, to that spectacular first glimpse of the soaring Rockies, or according to his maps, the Sierra Madres. "A grand bed of snowcapped mountains rose before us, pile upon pile, glowing in the bright light."

During the south leg of his second trip, Fremont and his guide Kit Carson sent Maxwell, a member of the party, south to Taos to purchase mules. He notes his fear that Maxwell might be captured by the "Yutes," who he feels are hostile to the expedition. Upon reaching South Park, the group finds the huge, grassy, highland basin, "alive with buffalo."

Fremont's party actually contacted the Utes at South Park. Approaching the area they met a group of beaver trappers and were warned that a band of Arapahoes had recently passed through the area on their way to attack a village of Utes. The next day, the Fremont party encountered a group of weeping and wailing Ute women. Through interpreters they learned that the Arapahoes had attacked the sleeping hunting camp at dawn that day and had killed several Ute leaders. Many Ute horses were driven off by the attackers and were herded into a carefully prepared fort nearby that was strongly defended. The women pleaded with Fremont to help the Utes drive off the Arapahoes and get their horses back. But Fremont realized the danger of taking sides in the conflict and refused to help. Later in the day, Fremont's scouts returned to camp to report that the Utes "seem to be getting the upper hand in the conflict and are driving the Arapahoes out of South Park."

Fortunately for the Utes, the rugged terrain of their mountain homeland and its severe weather, and the tribe's formidable reputation for protecting their ancestral territory, persuaded most of the growing wave of westward migrants to circumvent the Colorado highlands and keep away from Ute territory. Nonetheless, the proximity of so many potential invaders posed a threat to the independent and self-sufficient Utes, and the tribe tended to retreat deeper into their wild mountains.

The unpopular Mormons, followers of Joseph Smith and Brigham Young, had been driven from their Midwestern settlements in Ohio and Illinois. Guided partially by Fremont's journals, the homeless Mormons migrated westward until they finally reached the Great Salt Lake in 1847. Here they encountered bands of northern Utes and villages of Piutes near the lake shore. As was their tradition when in contact with whites, the Utes were generally peaceful, but at first were unwilling to accept coexistence with the Mormons. There was conflict in the beginning, but Brigham Young's wise policies of non-interference with the Indians, and his willingness to sell them guns, cemented a long friendship. Later, in explaining their good relationship with the Mormons to United States commissioners, the Utes pointedly said, "The Mormons keep their promises." The Mormons were not above proselytizing the Utes, however, and Chief Walkara, a powerful leader of the Salt Lake Ute band, was made an elder of the Mormon church. In conferring this honor, the Mormons first induced from him a reluctant promise to discontinue his habit of stealing Mormon horses and then selling them back to the Mormons. Walkara became a popular Ute leader partially due to his highly successful horse-stealing business. Although he was forced to make a tentative peace with the Mormons due to insistence by the rival and more moderate leader Souviette, Walkara still continued his lucrative partnership with a former fur trapper and mountain man, T. L. "Pegleg" Smith. Smith had lived among the Indians for years and had won their respect. He was considered strong and fearless, and it was said he had helped to cut off his own badly wounded leg. Raids south and westward into southern Utah and Nevada by Smith and Chief Walkara's large band of horse thieves had become big business, and their notoriety spread throughout the West.

Walkara's most spectacular raid occurred in 1840 when his large band of renegades made a long and difficult journey to the far-distant Pacific Coast, as far as the Spanish-Mexican settlement at San Bernardino, California. His band of Utes and other Indians raided throughout the area, eventually collecting between 2,000 and 3,000 horses for the return trip to the Salt Lake region. An estimated 2,000 stolen animals survived the hard trip back to Utah and were sold to trappers and Ute tribesmen in the area. Some of the same Spanish horses were eventually sold back to the Spanish at Santa Fe.

From 1830 to 1848 the enterprising Chief Walkara continued to collect tribute from caravans passing on their way westward. He even dabbled in the slave trade, capturing neighboring Piute girls for sale to the Spanish as household slaves. Indian slave trade was not new. It had been practiced for centuries as a natural product of war. In Utah the practice was finally legally banned by the territorial legislature in 1852.

John Fremont recalls in his journals his meeting with Chief "Walker," Walkara, of the Utes, in central Utah. He was impressed with the chief, and they exchanged gifts. Walkara admitted to Fremont that his well-armed party of warriors was on its way to intercept a Spanish caravan on its way to California through his territory. Walkara usually allowed the caravans to proceed westward peacefully if they agreed to pay him an adequate ransom, otherwise he attacked. Obviously, Chief Walkara died a rich a man.

After his death, Ute leadership in the Salt Lake region passed to Chiefs Souviette and Tabby, who proved to be more peaceful and pliable in their negotiations with the Mormons than Walkara had been. Eventually, a treaty was negotiated by the Mormon elders whereby the Utes living in the region agreed to leave the fast-developing Salt Lake Valley to occupy lands to the east in the region of the Uintah River. This group has since been known as the Uintah Utes.

Western Indians everywhere were beginning to feel the intense pressure of white settlement pushing from all sides. The various Ute bands were increasingly irritated by the encroachments, particularly in the rich San Luis Valley of south central Colorado that they had kept free of settlers for so long. Large land grants in the area were beginning to bring in Mexican Americans in numbers too great to be chased out. In order to protect these new settlers, the federal government in 1852 established the first strong fortification inside Ute territory. It was hastily built of pine logs laid side by side and named Fort Massachusetts. The first location of the new outpost in the San Luis Valley was considered poor because of defensive considerations and poor soil conditions, and it was soon moved to a wide section of the valley six miles from the original location and about 25 miles east of present Alamosa. The new encampment was renamed Fort Garland and was more permanently built of adobe brick plastered to a smooth finish. It was garrisoned from 1858 to 1883. Today, after extensive restoration, the fort can still be visited, looking very similar to its original condition in a great valley that appears much as it did 100 years ago.

The establishment of Fort Garland, garrisoned by regular uniformed United States troops and at one point commanded by Kit Carson, frightened and angered the Utes. Some of the younger tribal leaders counseled that the time had come to fight back in force and again drive the white men from the valley. After many years of general peace there were again sporadic attacks on new settlers in the area, quickly followed by counterattacks against the Indians. The so-called Ute War of 1854-55 had broken out.

On a cold Christmas Day, at an old trappers' outpost called Fort Napesta, newly arrived settlers were loudly celebrating the holiday. A few Capote Utes were visiting the lonely trading post and had been invited to join the festivities and, along with the trappers and frontiersmen, were getting good and drunk. At many wilderness outposts, liquor was the one universal cure for loneliness.

What actually occurred is not clear, but a band of Mouache Utes under the leadership of Tierra Blanca had, very pointedly, not been invited to the party, but came anyway with guns, bows and arrows, and war clubs. Aided by friends from a nearby Jicarilla Apache settlement, the Mouache war party soon captured the fortified trading post. Fifteen defenders were killed and one woman and two children were taken captive. History records that the rest of the holiday spirits were consumed by the uninvited Indians. Encouraged by the strong refreshment found at the fort, Tierra Blanca and his men continued on and attacked several nearby ranches. News of this serious Indian uprising was immediately spread by couriers to terrified ranch families throughout the San Luis Valley. Some settlers quickly packed their children and valuables and fled to safer, larger settlements. General Garland dispatched Colonel Thomas Fauntleroy in pursuit of Tierra Blanca and his band. The Utes learned that a large force was being gathered to pursue them and, by now somewhat sobered after their spontaneous escapade, they soon disappeared in the hills.

Finally, in April, after much unsuccessful searching, six companies of mounted volunteers plus regular army units sighted an Indian war party near Cochetopa Pass. The war leader Tierra Blanca was easily recognized among them by the bright red shirt that he always wore. The small army of men gave vigorous pursuit but again the Indians simply seemed to disappear into the rugged brush-filled hill country. Sometime later, Colonel Fauntleroy with Kit Carson as his guide caught up with another armed Ute band near Salida, Colorado. This time the Indians were soundly defeated and lost about 40 of their group and a herd of stolen cattle. Cattle stealing had rarely been a serious problem before this date in Ute history. But due to the senseless slaughter of the once vast buffalo herds by white commercial hunters, so-called sportsmen, and settlers, some Indians had been driven to prey upon the cattle herds in order to obtain much-needed supplies of hides and meat.

This series of episodes tragically reminded the Indians again that the white soldiers with their superior weapons and larger numbers of men could not be permanently defeated. The Utes soon agreed to sign a new peace treaty ending the short period of hostility. This was the Treaty of 1855, and it seems to have greatly influenced the pacifist tendencies of a young and intelligent Ute leader named Ouray, who was soon to become the principal Ute chieftain. Some isolated hostilities continued, usually provoked by aggressive or reckless migrants and travelers. Generally though, there was peace again with the Ute bands throughout the Colorado Rockies.

In 1853, Captain John Gunnison crossed Ute territory on a mission approved by Secretary of War Jefferson C. Davis. Captain Gunnison was ordered to map possible routes for a transcontinental railroad to link the eastern states with the new California gold fields. About this same time anonymous immigrants who were traveling through Utah on their way west needlessly murdered peaceful members of the Piute tribe they encountered along the trail. A vengeful party of Piutes, by accident, discovered the Gunnison survey party near the Colorado-Utah border.

At dawn the Gunnison party was preparing breakfast on a relatively flat valley plain. There was plenty of open space in all directions, and it had seemed a good place to set up a survey camp. Coffee has just been prepared when out of the surrounding sagebrush rose a screaming war party of angry Piutes. They had crawled for some distance through the brush to the very edge of the camp in the darkness before dawn. Captain Gunnison and members of his party were easily killed, and only those who were able to reach their horses escaped. One survivor was thrown from his horse while riding away, but managed to hide in the brush until he was rescued. Captain Gunnison was found pierced by 15 arrows, and some of the bodies had been hacked to pieces to insure that they could not go to the "Happy Hunting Ground."

The unprovoked attack was apparently in retaliation for the previous murder of Piutes. The Gunnison party was guided by one Le Roux, a well-known trapper and guide. He had been apprehensive about

Rare photo of a Ute warrior in full war paint. Photo by the Powell Survey.

entering Ute and Piute territory due to a previous incident in which he had killed a Ute tribesman whom he accused of stealing his horse. Before the attack, Le Roux held a lengthy powwow to make peace with the Utes when they had recently visited the Gunnison camp.

The journal also notes that the Utes had been willing to sell horses to the survey party only in exchange for gunpowder and lead, and that near the Grand River, a campfire left by the Gunnison party had started a bad brush fire. Whether any of these incidents had a bearing on the later Piute attack is unknown.

Captain Gunnison's survey party had already mapped vast sections of the western slope of the Rockies and had made notes regarding the possibility of rich mineral deposits in the vicinity of the Roaring Fork and Crystal River valleys. His notes were highly valuable to later survey parties in the region.

CHIEF OURAY, THE ARROW, AND THE TREATY MAKERS

By 1860, the year before the Civil War started, the Ute people were attempting to isolate themselves from the outside world. Despite the continual pressure on their valley campsites, they could still avoid most contact with the strange and dangerous new civilization by retreating into the heart of their Rocky Mountain domain. More and more, they chose to hunt in summer in the high country of central Colorado because the herds of game were also being frightened and pushed into more remote mountain habitats. Ute winter encampments became more remote too. Larger groups wintered in the Gunnison River Valley and in the isolated western-slope valleys near present Montrose and Grand Junction.

The final end to the primeval privacy of the Ute people occurred suddenly, just before the Civil War began. In 1858 placer gold was discovered on Cherry Creek near the eastern foothills of the Colorado Rockies. The first gold was found in river-bed gravel, and it indicated the possibility of rich mother lode deposits at the source of the creek in the Ute-held high country. Within a mere 30 years, a large area near the spot where little Cherry Creek enters the foothills was covered with homes and boarding houses and hotels, and the streets were busy with dry goods stores and lumber yards; this new city was called Denver. Within a shorter 22 years, the Utes were removed from the Colorado high country and became a mere memory throughout most of the state.

The first significant evidence of Colorado gold was discovered by a small group of prospectors while traveling west from the state of Georgia where they had been prospecting near Dahlonega, the site of the first major gold discovery in the United States. Among this group of gold seekers were several Cherokee Indians. The Georgia gold deposits played out quickly, and the men were apparently on their way to California to try the new high Sierra gold fields. Recognizing favorable gravel deposits as they crossed Cherry Creek, they decided to try a little panning before continuing west into the mountains. It's ironic that Indian propsectors were involved in the final opening of Ute territory, one of the last, vast, exclusively Indian domains in the territorial United States.

By the following summer, 50,000 people had hastily left their homes in the eastern states and joined the rush to "Pikes Peak," as the entire region was then called. Traveling by horse, covered wagon, mule, ox-cart, canoe, and flat boat, and even on foot pushing wheelbarrows loaded with supplies, they came to the country where the rivers and streams were reported to be lined with gleaming gold.

In 1859 at Denver, the *Rocky Mountain News* ran the complete text of the new constitution for the territory, then called The Territory of Jefferson. The frontier town quickly grew from a tent city frequently visited by curious Kiowas, Cheyennes, Arapahoes, and Sioux into a full-fledged metropolis of two-story brick and frame buildings.

The Denver gold strike was significant, but a little way up Clear Creek near present Idaho Springs just west of Denver, gloriously rich sediments of placer gold were found. Soon deep veins of gold-bearing rock were discovered in formations on the cliffsides, the mother lodes. The stampede to Ute country was on.

Hard-working Horace Tabor, a small-time grocer, trudged up Ute Pass from Colorado City (now Colorado Springs) to the gold camps in South Park. It took him two weeks at five miles a day with a wagonload of flour, sugar, pork, and other trade goods. By means of shrewd investing and by backing others with credit, he was soon to become one of Colorado's most flamboyant mining tycoons. The following year, 1860, an important gold strike was made at California Gulch, and 5,000 would-be miners scrambled and crawled over the Continental Divide to found the city of Leadville at the hard-breathing elevation of 10,000 feet above sea level.

Regardless of the sensational stories about Indian dangers that were constantly printed in eastern newspapers, there was very little armed resistance by the Utes to this sudden foreign invasion. In 1859, prospectors dug for 16 days deep inside Ute territory at the headwaters of the Grand River before being discovered and driven out by Indian threats. Near Auraria the same year near Denver, prospectors were suddenly attacked and a Dr. Schunk was killed, but it is doubtful the attack was by Utes.

Exaggerated tales of Indian murders and scalpings had been reported, true or false, by an unscrupulous press, tantilizing their readers with bloody adventure stories in order to sell newspapers. Many newly arrived fortune hunters climbed the mysterious Rocky Mountains expecting to find wild, murderous Indians behind every rock. Guns were carried as standard equipment, and some travelers would shoot at any Indian seen on the trail before trying to make friends. The peaceful intentions of the Utes, who simply wanted to be left alone, were being strained to the limit. The younger men again talked of taking action in order to drive out the white hordes who were rapidly killing the diminishing supplies of game. The Utes needed a strong, new leader.

Chief Nevava of the Tabeguache (Uncompahgre) band was the most influential Ute leader of the period, but he was aging and finally died in his teepee in 1859. Nevava had taken part in the first treaty signed with the United States at Abiquiu. He watched helplessly as more and more foreigners moved onto his people's hunting lands, running the deer and decimating the buffalo herds. Some of his good friends had been senselessly killed, while others had been threatened and driven away from favorite camping sites.

Shortly before his death, the old chief was visited by Ouray, "the arrow," son of Guera Morah, a leader sometimes called Salvadore by the Spanish. Ouray was young and vigorous, and he argued eloquently that the Utes must seek a new, more binding treaty with the United States government in order to protect their threatened homeland. Chief Nevava refused to take part in new negotiations, saying that many tribes had learned that the white man's treaties were worthless. He reminded Ouray that even when agreements were signed in good faith, the government soldiers could not control their own people.

Ouray had recently visited the gold camps and the huge new tent city at Denver, and he told Nevava of the great masses of migrants moving westward. He told of seeing more white people in a single camp than there ever had been Utes together. Still Nevava refused to act. Finally, after long debate among the elders, Ouray, who was becoming a

Christopher "Kit" Carson—one of the last photos, made during his eastern trip with the Ute delegation in 1868. He died during the return trip.

fine orator, was able to pursuade the tribal council of the importance of obtaining a new protective treaty for their people.

Ouray was dispatched by the council on a long horseback trip to Santa Fe. He spoke four languages, including Ute, Apache, Spanish, and English, and during many future negotiations in which Ouray was destined to take part, his linguistic skill proved to be a valuable asset. Ouray sought out "Rope Thrower" Kit Carson upon his arrival in the old Spanish territorial capital. Carson was a long-time friend of the Utes, and despite his occasional moves against other tribes, he was still trusted by the Utes. The Ouray delegation requested that Carson set up new treaty negotiations between the U.S. government and the various Ute bands in order to stop the invasion of Ute lands by settlers and prospectors.

Ouray, a member of the Uncompahgre Utes, was one of those exceptional Indians who stands out even in terms of the leadership criteria of western civilization. During his lifetime he was to win the intellectual respect of even his most critical adversaries. Ouray possessed a sophisticated understanding of the kind of diplomatic pragmatism that was necessary to deal with the new incoming civilization and was so essential to guide his people towards eventual acceptance of the strange requirements of the twentieth century.

Biographers and chroniclers of American history have given lasting recognition to only a thin handful of Indian leaders who represented tribes east of the Mississippi River, in spite of several hundred years of intimate exposure to them long before white men began to explore the West. Tecumseh of the Shawnees, and Joseph Brant, the Mohawk evangelist who became a renowned missionary, and of course Sequoyah, who devised the only North American Indian written language in a belated attempt to preserve the records and ideas of his Cherokee people—these men and few other Indians became lasting American heros. It is significant, in our limited knowledge of primeval Indian history, that two of these three leaders were part Caucasian and thus more acceptable and easily understood by historians.

Intellectual contacts with the tribes west of the Mississippi River were rare until the reservation period. Western Indian culture had entered its final stage of decline before serious writers, painters, photographers, and anthropologists began to take a close look at the western tribes. Therefore, the careers and ability of most western Indian leaders have been preserved only through storytelling and myth. Those few western Indian leaders who did receive adequate coverage in the history books have been ranked more in terms of their military prowess and their effect on the western migration. The records rarely relfect their true reputation in the eyes of their own people.

Much of the reponsibility for this obscurity of leadership was the result of Indian society itself. There was no chieftain class. In fact chiefs in the popular sense of the word were rare. A leader would emerge out of the tribal councils more or less by default, and the power of any leader was strictly limited by the essential continued respect of his people. History tends to remember outstanding war leaders, but such men were often not chiefs and in most cases had very little influence over tribal affairs except in battle. This was true of battle leaders such as Geronimo of the Chiricahua Apaches and Captain Jack, the northern Ute leader during the battle of Milk Creek.

The only great Ute leader whose character and personality was fairly well interpreted and recorded for history was Ouray, "the arrow." Ouray was born about 1833 near Taos, New Mexico. His father was Guera Murah, a half-Ute, half-Jicarilla Apache who married a Tabeguache Ute. In normal Indian tradition, Guera Murah joined his wife's family group and was later adopted into the Ute tribe. Soon he became a leader of the Tabeguache band.

For reasons that remain unclear, Ouray was placed with a well-to-do Spanish ranching family near Taos as a child and worked as a sheepherder. Since early Spanish colonial times, many Indian children were sold or bartered into service with Spanish families as indentured servants. Sometimes surplus or even favorite children were simply loaned by Indian families to be raised and educated in the white man's world, in exchange for work. Although Ouray could neither read nor write, he did manage to learn to speak four languages while growing up. When he reached 18 years of age, the lure of his father's free, independent life proved too much to resist, and Ouray ran away to join his father's people. Old Guera Murah had become the principal leader of the Tabeguaches and soon after being reunited with his son, the old man died. Before his death he gave Ouray 12 horses, a very sizable inheritance for a young Indian.

The Tabeguaches lived in south central Colorado, close to the great buffalo herds that roamed the vast grasslands to the east. They had become excellent buffalo hunters, and as the great herds diminished,

Chief Ouray (the Arrow) in buckskin shirt. This photo was taken during the Utes' last treaty negotiations at Washington, D.C. in 1880, only months before Ouray's death.

hunting sometimes necessitated dangerous trips onto the eastern plains of Colorado to track the smaller and more elusive herds. Occasionally when hunting was bad, these trips required travel into far-off western Kansas and the Oklahoma panhandle.

The vast grassy plains east of the Rockies traditionally belonged to the hostile Sioux, Arapahoes, Cheyennes, Kiowas, Comanches, and other tribes, and the long hunting trips were accompanied by the risk of attack. On one such expedition, Ouray was accompanied by his first wife and his five-year-old son, Queashegut, sometimes called Cotsan. One day a surprise attack was made on the Ute hunting camp by a war party of Arapahoes, near Ft. Lupton, Colorado. At the time of the attack, most of the Utes hunters including Ouray were away from the camp and separated from the women and children. Ouray's only son was captured and carried off on horseback by an Arapahoe warrior. For many years Ouray attempted to locate his lost son. During treaty negotiations with the U.S. government years later, he happened to mention the story to Felix Brunot of the Bureau of Indian Affairs. Through various Indian agents Brunot attempted to locate the boy among the Arapahoe villages. After long investigation a young man was found who according to reports had been stolen from the Utes as a child and evidence indicated that this was Ouray's son. But, when the young man discovered that his true father was a Ute, he refused to meet Ouray until finally pursuaded to do so by Brunot. The meeting was not a success. The young Arapahoe would not acknowledge the relationship, nor would he ever admit that he could have been born into the hated Ute tribe.

Ouray later married Chipeta, a beautiful young Tabeguache girl with slanting oriental eyes. She was eventually to become as well known as her famous husband, and lived past 80 years, dying in 1924. Although she had many white friends some of whom tended to use her as a "cause celebre" or symbol of her people, Chipeta never accepted the many offers to live with them, choosing instead to stay with her own people. Ouray was considered unusually "civilized" for an Indian, and although he was without formal education, his personality and manner displayed exceptional dignity and charm. He was 5 feet 7 inches and of stocky build. His voice, like most Utes, was low and soft, yet unusually commanding. He loved lengthy conversation and never failed to charm the many government representatives who called upon him. Even in Washington, D.C., he was considered an outstanding speaker. In his later years, Ouray and Chipeta lived in a cabin built for them by the government. Unlike Chipeta, Ouray seemed to prefer to wear yankee clothing on formal occasions, although this could have been another display of his renowned diplomacy.

Ouray became the principal leader of the Tabeguache band after the retirement of Nevava, and he soon won the unqualified admiration of Colonel Kit Carson during the treaty negotiations of 1859. Although he was later considered by the U.S. government to be the chief of all the Utes, Ouray was never accepted as supreme chief by all of the Ute bands. There had never been a supreme Ute chief. Such centralized power was foreign to the Utes, and to this day some members of the tribe find Ouray's career controversial due to his willingness to compromise with the U.S. government.

Very few Indian tribes had a tradition of a principal chief except in war. They could not understand why one leader of one band should take precedence over leaders of other bands, regardless of superior ability. Despite this, Ouray's strong personality and backing by the government enabled him to exert extensive power over most of the tribe. Yet there were times of dissension and jealously even among members of his own Tabeguache band. This led to at least one conspiracy to replace him as leader. Chipeta's feisty, jealous brother Sapawanero was apparently persuaded by other conspirators to attempt to murder his powerful brother-in-law. After lengthy plotting, the dissidents arranged an ambush. One day as Ouray led his horse into the blacksmith's shop at the Los Pinos agency, Sapawanero, who was standing in the dark interior of the building, lunged at him wielding an ax. Ouray's life was saved by a gesture from the blacksmith, who had anticipated the attack. He was barely able to dodge behind a nearby tree as the ax handle broke harmlessly against the tree trunk. The stronger Ouray grabbed Sapawanero by the shoulders and flung him into a ditch. As Ouray furiously reached for his knife to kill his attacker. Chipeta rushed up and deftly removed the weapon from its sheath at her husband's waist. Before this incongruous attack and even shortly thereafter, Sapawanero was Ouray's most trusted lieutenant and was often left as acting Tabeguache chief during his brother-in-law's frequent absences.

Ouray fought several duels with opponents of his leadership policies, and he continued to anger some by his friendship with government authorities. His wisdom regarding the best interests of his people and his cool judgment of the white man's overwhelming power never waivered. Ouray used his friendly contacts with the government to maximum advantage. His intelligence impressed all who met him, including President Rutherford Hayes, who made the enthusiastic comment to friends that "Ouray is the most intellectual man I have ever conversed with." During the entire period of his leadership, Ouray insisted that his people keep the peace, realizing that to fight the overwhelming wave of western migration with guns meant virtual annihilation of the Indians. He shrewdly negotiated a long series of largely beneficial treaties, achieving a record of success equalled by few other tribes.

In 1868, at the zenith of his power, Ouray succeeded in negotiating a treaty considered to be one of the most favorable ever won from the United States government by an Indian tribe. The treaty in effect barred all whites from entering the western slope of the Colorado Rockies and even dislodged many prospectors who were already there. Ouray won, almost singlehandedly, 12 years of additional freedom for his people, at a time when most tribes had reluctantly accepted reservation life. Ouray had no illusions about the capricious nature of the U.S. government. Once, to illustrate his lasting frustration with the unreliable attitudes of the U.S. Congress, he told reporters, "Agreements the Indian makes with the government are like the agreement a buffalo makes with the hunter after it has been pierced by many arrows. All it can do is lie down and give in."

Chief Ouray loved to make hunting trips into his beloved Rocky Mountains with Chipeta and a few friends. For years he suffered from rheumatism and nephritis and took frequent trips to the hot springs located in the Ute territory on the western slope. As he approached middle age, he was increasingly in pain and was in poor health when, in 1879, he received word of the violent uprising against Agent Nathan Meeker at the White River Agency. He became uncharacteristically despondent concerning the actions of the northern Ute bands during this incident. He recognized that the resultant killings were a fatal error in judgment on the part of the medicine man Johnson and on the part of Colorow and Douglas, the northern Ute leaders. Ouray realized that his lifelong efforts to maintain peace with the government without giving up all precious land holdings and hunting privileges in the new State of Colorado were now inevitably to be destroyed. In desperation, he briefly considered joining the angry insurrection among the northern White River dissidents. Then, wisely, he dispatched a runner to the fleeing northern band demanding their surrender and an immediate release of the hostages they had taken during their retreat.

Ouray knew the White River incident, known as the Meeker Massacre, would provide the excuse needed to end Ute hunting rights in western Colorado. Following the uprising and lengthy government investigative hearings, the great chief managed to save the lives of his people, including even the guilty northern Ute leaders. Wasted by progressive illness, he died in pain only a year later at the age of 47. Ouray had counselled and led his people well. During 20 years of dominance over his tribe, he had personally matched wits with members of the U.S. Congress, the Army, Secretary of the Interior Carl Schurz, Felix Brunot of the Bureau of Indian Affairs, Generals McCook and Adams, Colonel Kit Carson, Governors John Evans, Henry Pitkin, and Henry Teller, and Presidents U.S. Grant and Rutherford Hayes. He always emerged from these contests with more advantage for his "Blue Sky People" than anyone had thought possible. Chief Ouray died one of the most admired men during the tragic destruction of western Indian culture. He was truly one of the great leaders of his time.

By 1863, gold seekers and Civil War veterans, deserters, and refugees trying to escape the war were flooding into Colorado as never before. Seven separate Indian agencies were operated by the government to serve the Utes and other nearby tribes with enough supplies to keep them quiet. Despite all efforts, friction between the two worlds was rapidly increasing. A new agency had recently opened for the northern Utes at Hot Sulphur Springs, Colorado. Another Indian agency at faraway Denver had previously served several tribes, including the Tabeguache Ute band; now a new agency was being opened at Conejos, closer to the Utes home country. There was a sub-agency located on the huge Maxwell land grant near Cimarron, New Mexico, for the Mouache Utes. The Capotes were still contacted and served at the Abiquiu agency and the Weeminuches were supplied at Tierra Amarilla. The Taos agency served serveral tribes but continued to keep track of other miscellaneous southern Utes.

A conference to discuss territorial boundaries as Ouray had requested from Colonel Carson, was called at Conejos in 1863, but only the Tabeguaches showed up in sufficient numbers to negotiate. Fear and mistrust of the U.S. authorities was growing among most of the Ute bands. Nonetheless, under the firm leadership of Ouray, a treaty was signed at the Conejos conference defining territorial boundaries for the

Gen. Edward McCook, appointed Colorado Territorial Governor by President Grant, his comrade at Shiloh. McCook was noted for nepotism in office; nonetheless, he appointed a successful Ute agent, Charles Adams, his brother-in-law.

Tabeguache Utes for the first time. Their land began at the source of the Uncompaghre River, ran northwest to present Grand Junction, then up the Colorado River to the site of Glenwood Springs and south up the Roaring Fork River close to Aspen, then south along the Sawatch Range to the Sangre de Christos, and west to the Rio Grande. The treaty called for annual gifts to the tribe of cattle, sheep, $10,000 annually in cash, $10,000 worth of provisions, and a new blacksmith shop. As a finale to the conference Ouray and the Tabeguache leaders were presented with silver medals.

The government failed to honor even the first payments under the new treaty. The treaty negotiators' efforts although sincere were frustrated by a Civil-War-obsessed Congress that simply failed to pass the necessary appropriations. As Horace Greeley stated in a letter to a friend, "The skies are dark, we are threatened with Copperhead rebellion and foreign intervention and we are dying of enormous debt and taxation." There just wasn't time to worry about the rights of a little tribe of Indians in far-off Colorado territory.

By 1868, settlement of the agriculturally rich San Luis Valley had grown to the point where the Indians and settlers could not longer live side by side. The American Civil War had finally ended, and thousands of homeless veterans headed west to the gold fields. It was time to again think about a full-blown treaty with all the Utes. It took a lot of persuading and gift giving but finally, following much fanfair and pomp, representatives of the seven Ute bands, dressed in their finest attire, were transported by rail all the way to Washington, D.C., for a formal conference. The Tabeguaches, Mouaches, Capotes, Weeminuches, Yampas, Grand River, and Uintahs were all represented. To make the shy Utes feel more comfortable in this strange environment, their old friend "Rope Thrower" was named chief government negotiator, and Ouray was formally recognized by the government as the principal Ute chief, despite old jealousies. After being paraded around Washington and shown the sights, the conference got under way. There was an abundance of oratory on both sides, and it was finally agreed that a single territorial allotment, including most of the western third of Colorado, would be set aside as exclusive Ute territory. No white man was to enter this vast area without Ute permission. The Uintah reservation east of Salt Lake had already been defined by Congress in 1864 and remained separate and unchanged. The new territory including approximately 16 million acres served a Ute population of probably 4,000. The eastern boundary of this newly defined Colorado Ute territory ran north to south from near present-day Steamboat Springs to Basalt, Crested Butte, Gunnison, and over the San Juan Mountains to Pagosa Springs, and on to the border of New Mexico. On the west, the boundary was the Utah line. The treaty also provided for educational facilities, land allotments in severalty, and $60,000 per year in clothing, blankets, and food until the Utes should become self-sufficient on their own lands. Subsequently, the Treaty of 1868 was ratified by the U.S. Senate. The shy Weeminuches, who had lived mainly in southeastern Utah, objected vehemently to being forced to move back into Colorado. A majority, but not all, finally moved to the vicinity of Los Pinos agency. Some under their leader Cabeza Blanca peaceably continued to resist the move and remained in southern Utah. Many of their descendants still reside in the vicinity of Blanding, Utah, where they have successfully integrated themselves among their white neighbors.

Chief Ouray insisted that the Treaty of 1868 be made binding and "final forever," and the government solemnly agreed. Yet the terms of this important agreement were honored by the government for only five years.

The Los Pinos Agency was built in Saguache County, Colorado, for the purpose of distributing treaty goods to the Tabeguache Utes and also to try to keep the Indians peacefully within the boundaries of Ute lands. Many Indian agencies historically had been administered by powerful missionary branches of various Christian church groups, and competition became keen between the religious denominations for these franchises from God. The second administrative agent sent to operate the Los Pinos Agency was one Reverend Jabez Nelson Trask from Boston. Reverend Trask was appointed and sent west by the Unitarian Church of Massachusetts, causing some cynics to claim that the Unitarians liked to help the Indians because Unitarians only felt comfortable with heathens. Reverend Trask represented a type of administration that had become familiar to many Indian agencies. He was strong-willed, a recent product of Harvard University and Cambridge Divinity School. The new administrator to the southern Utes was also extremely confident of his righteousness and comfortably narrow in his views. Downright eccentric by most standards, the strange behavior of Reverend Trask greatly amused some of the Indians but deeply angered others. The new administrator was conscientious to the point of embarrassment, so much so that the Indians soon tired of his queer ideas and went to great lengths to ignore his presence. The situation deteriorated until finally the Utes could stand the situation no longer. A powwow was held and the elders of the tribe formally sent a request to the government asking that Reverend Trask be replaced. Their grievances were lengthy and among other things listed his stinginess, his stubborn refusal to associate with the Indians, and his arrogant, superior attitude. After one long, trying year on the job, Trask and his family moved back East, and his replacement took over the Los Pinos Agency. Years later, the Reverend Trask in a typical fervor of enthusiasm executed a last will and testament leaving his entire estate to the Society for the Protection of Dumb Animals.

General Charles Adams' subsequent appointment as administrator of the Los Pinos Agency was greeted with pleasure by the Indians. He was General of Territorial Militia and had known the Utes on a friendly basis for many years, having served at Fort Union, Colorado, and in New Mexico. He had a good knowledge of Indian problems, understood the Ute people well, and respected them. Unfortunately, too many agents and missionaries of the period lacked even a basic understanding of Indian life and tended to treat their charges like unruly children.

General Adams was equally well thought of by the Navajos and the Apaches. He was German by birth and came to his new job highly recommended by General McCook, governor of the Colorado territory. His beginning and ending salary was $1,500 per year, plus his wife's meager earnings as the agency teacher. Adams and his wife served well, and through their efforts most of the terms of the 1868 treaty were carried out during their term of duty. Supplies of blankets, utensils, and food were laboriously hauled by wagon to the Los Pinos Agency by a former fur trapper and trader, Otto Mears, under contract with the government. The story of Otto Mears, a Russian-born Jewish immigrant who became a leading Colorado pioneer and road builder, is a fascinating tale in itself. Finally, the administration at Los Pinos was accomplishing its purpose.

The Los Pinos Agency was running well when, one dark day, a letter arrived from Washington, D.C., for General Adams and his wife, telling a sad story of political revenge. By careful sleuthing, the good Unitarians back in Boston had discovered that General Adams was Catholic. Panic seized the congregation. Galled by the failure of their former representative, Reverend Trask, the vengeful church leaders contacted their political allies in Washington. Visions of innocent Unitarian Indians being prosyletized by the wily Pope were too terrible to contemplate, and in 1875, the popular General Adams and his wife were "sacked." Actually, the good Unitarians need not have worried. After centuries of limited exposure to the conversion-minded Spanish padres, hardly a "Hail Mary" could be heard throughout the entire Ute tribe. (Actually, a few successful conversions were made to Catholicism over the years.)

As if to purge the recent "unfortunate" influence, another Harvard Theological graduate soon appeared at the Los Pinos Agency, Bible in hand, to administer his superior knowledge to the unfortunate Indians. He was known as Reverend Henry Bond. Fortunately for all, Reverend Bond's tenure was also short-lived. A shortage in the government cattle allotment funds was discovered, and his resignation was hastily requested. Before the Bond family left, the agency received a visit from famed western photographer, William Henry Jackson.

Jackson had accompanied Dr. Hayden, a geological surveyor for the Department of the Interior, on several mapping trips into the Rockies. In his biography he tells of his trip to the Indian agency at Los Pinos.

In late August, with a photographic party of seven including packers, assistants, a cook, and a complete darkroom, W. H. Jackson traveled from Clear Creek Canyon past Middle Park then south to San Luis Park and west to the San Juans. He crossed Cochetopa Pass through forests of aspen and spruce to Los Pinos Creek. At the agency he found 70 Uncompahgre (Tabeguache) Ute teepees spread over the meadow surrounded by hundreds of Indian ponies. According to Jackson, the resident administrator, Reverend Bond, seemed particularly crestfallen when he discovered that Jackson had traveled the long distance simply to photograph the Indians and not Reverend Bond and his family.

Jackson was introduced to Chief Ouray and photographed the leader's new adobe home that had been built for him by General Adams under terms of the treaty agreement. Jackson, too, comments about Ouray's "urbane friendliness and keen intelligence." He describes Ouray as rather shorter and more heavyset than most Utes and with a large head and fine features. "He lives austerely, uses no tobacco, and hates whiskey," according to Jackson.

Jackson immediately set up his bulky equipment and began to photograph Ouray and Chipeta and her brother, Piah, whom he describ-

William H. Jackson, famous western photographer, checking a wet plate outside his portable darkroom. His equipment was carried by donkey and wagon to the Ute reservation.

ed as a great subject. Suddenly, an autumn afternoon thunderstorm interrupted the photographic session and brought with it superstition. The next day Jackson and his party were formally introduced to the assembled Ute leaders by Agent Reverend Bond. In accordance with tribal etiquette he was then led into a teepee for the traditional pipe smoking. After the friendly ceremony, he was politely informed that a Ute medicine man had decided there should be no more pictures taken. Both Shavano and Guerro among the elders gravely informed Jackson that his mysterious black box would make Indians "heap sick," "make squaw die, papoose die, all die," "No Bueno."

No amount of persuasion seemed to have any effect on the decision of the elders. Jackson tried flattery and even bought blankets from the Indians. In desperation, he tried to photograph surreptitiously only to have the black cloth hood pulled off his camera and to find Indians standing in front of his subject with their backs to the camera. Later, during his return trip toward Denver, Jackson again tried to photograph Utes he encountered on the way with equally poor results.

A famous artist visited the Southern Ute Reservation, which by 1893 was headquartered at Ignacio, Colorado. Charles Schreyvogel was invited by Dr. McDonald, the Indian agent at the time, to include the Ute reservation on his five-month tour among the southwestern tribes. Unfortunately, Schreyvogel was more fascinated by the classic, romantic portrayal of the U.S. Cavalry than by the Indians, and like Frederic Remington, his work glorifies the solders but more or less ignores the Indians. His paintings of Utes do little to increase our knowledge of them.

It seemed that the entire Ute tribe was in a bad frame of mind during the early 1870s. There had been a much-publicized attack on the Gardner-Gennett survey party by renegade Utes near Sierra Abajo on the Mancos River. No one was killed but the people had become deeply distressed by the intrusion of so many survey teams into Indian territory, disturbing the game and violating the new treaty agreements that were supposedly "final and forever."

Major John Wesley Powell and his government-sponsored survey party mapped 900 miles of the Colorado River in 1869, shooting treacherous rapids in small wooden boats despite the fact that Powell had lost an arm at the battle of Shiloh. He visited with many parties of Utes and spent time at Douglas's encampment on the White River, where he studied the Ute language with the old northern Ute chief.

Dr. F. V. Hayden, chief of the Geological Survey, and his party of which W. H. Jackson was a part, obtained a special pass to cross Ute territory in 1873. They surveyed the western slope of the Colorado Rockies in detail, including the Crystal River Valley above Carbondale, which they declared to be one of the most complex geological formations in the world, bearing a record number of valuable minerals. Benjamin Graham and others had slipped into Ute territory previously and had prospected sites near present Carbondale, where they reported finding galena and rich coal deposits. Chief Colorow, whose clan of northern Utes spent each summer hunting in the beautiful Roaring Fork Valley between Glenwood Springs and Aspen, discovered the Graham party one day, poaching game. The Indians reminded the Graham party of the recent treaty and promptly drove them out of the area, burning all of their belongings.

By 1873, the slowly shrinking Ute nation was estimated to include 3,500 to 4,000 people still more or less divided into seven bands or clans. There was much anger expressed in the newspapers of the day, in response to complaints by hordes of mineral-hungry prospectors, over the fact that a handful of "ignorant savage Utes" still controlled the western third of Colorado territory.

Five short years after western Colorado was officially ceded to the Utes, it became obvious that the infiltration of gold and silver prospectors and settlers onto the western slope of the Rockies could not be stopped. An especially serious problem was intensifying in the San Juan mountain region of southwestern Colorado, where impressive gold strikes had been made in the vicinity of Silverton. Twice federal troops stationed at Fort Garland were dispatched to persuade the newly arrived and belligerent prospectors to leave Indian territory, but the attempts to uphold the treaty agreements were halfhearted and ultimately unsuccessful.

Finally, in 1872, new negotiations were started with Chief Ouray to persuade the elders of the tribe to cede the ore-rich San Juan Mountains to the United States. Angrily, Ouray reminded the Indian commissioners of their numerous promises and solemnly signed treaty commitments. This new conference ended in complete failure. Next, the Department of the Interior decided to try a more subtle approach. General Charles Adams, the former Catholic Indian agent at Los Pinos, was authorized to bring a delegation of Utes to Washington to meet General Grant.

General Adams was trusted by the elders, and 10 tribal members including Ouray, Chipeta (Ouray's wife), and Sapawanero were persuaded to make the long railroad trip. The party was accompanied by their old

Dr. Ferdinand V. Hayden and his survey party in camp in 1872. As chief geologist of the U.S. Geological and Geographical Survey he mapped the untold riches of Ute territory.

friend, trapper and scout Otto Mears, who acted as interpreter. The trip was well reported by newspapers throughout the East. The delegates were entertained well and visited New York City, Boston, Baltimore, and Philadelphia. The shy mountain people were expected to be impressed by the overwhelming power of this new civilization and undoubtedly the trip had the desired effect even though this was the second trip east for Ouray. The Indians were taken to see a circus, which they enjoyed, and visited the Cental Park Zoo, where they were greatly amused by the elephants. A newspaper announced that the Utes referred to elephants as those animals with "tails at both ends." A theatrical performance of the thriller "The Black Crook" didn't seem to impress the Utes much.

The government encouraged circulation throughout the Ute villages of reports about Chief Ouray's exciting adventures in the eastern cities. Then in August, 1873, the government insisted that a new council be held, headed by Felix Brunot, chief of the Indian commissioners. During lengthy meetings Otto Mears explained to Ouray the inability of the government to control the migration of men to the San Juan gold camps. He said, "It is much better sometimes to do what does not please us now, if it will be best for our children later." Brunot promised the government would set aside a large sum of money for the Utes and that interest on the money could be drawn by them annually. To this, a wise Ouray replied, "I would rather have all the money in the bank."

The complicated negotiations lasted for seven days. Many tribal elders did not wish to agree to any additional concessions, and there was angry debate. Reluctantly, the council recognized the inevitable and voted to cede the San Juans to the United States government for the purposes of mining operations only. The tribe managed to retain the right to hunt peacefully in the region. Known as the Brunot Treaty, this agreement gave up about 4 million additional acres, or one-fourth of the remaining Ute land in Colorado.

Again showing shrewdness in negotiations, Ouray managed to maintain intact for his people the bulk of a vast acreage on the western slope of Colorado. There had been no war as so often occurred before negotiations with others tribes. Surprisingly, it was now late in the 19th century, a full generation or more after most western tribes had been forceably driven from their native lands into far-removed reservations; yet the relatively small, tough tribe of Ute Indians was still proprietor of 12 million acres of their original homeland.

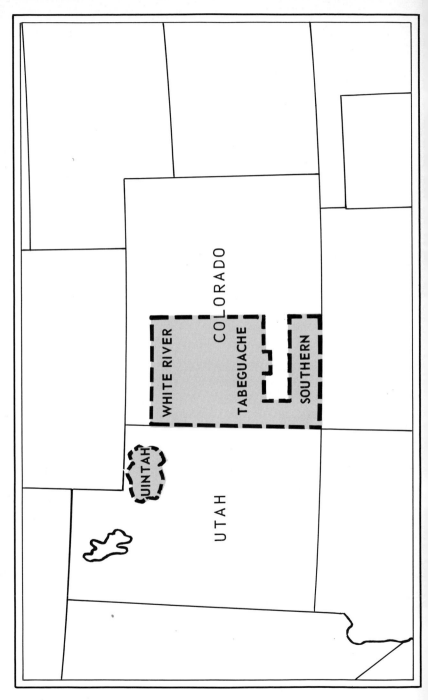

Delegates to the Brunot Treaty Conference of 1873: *third row, L. to R.,*
Washington, in his beloved uniform; Susan, Ouray's sister; Johnson, the medicine man
who fought Meeker; Nicaagat, war leader at Milk Creek; John; *second row, L. to R.,* Uriah
Curtis; Maj. J.B. Thompson; Gen. Charles Adams, Ute agent and friend; Otto Mears,
Pioneer and negotiator; *first row, L. to R.,* Guero; Chipeta, wife of Ouray; Chief Ouray;
and Piah, his brother-in-law.

Gov. Frederick W. Pitkin, a lawyer who came to Colorado for his health. He used demogogic fear of the Utes to propel himself into office and then tried to drive them from the state.

THE UTES MUST GO

The population of Colorado was now increasing so rapidly that a campaign for statehood had begun. Inevitably, the Brunot Treaty did not silence the rising cries against the Utes. "The Utes Must Go" was the merciless, growing chant in the Denver press. William B. Vickers, an ambitious, rather unscrupulous reporter for the *Denver Tribune*, mounted a personal campaign to rid Colorado of "the Ute Menace." Stories of Ute stealing and alleged murder, whether true or not, sold newspapers and were printed with increasing frequency. There was rarely much effort made to verify the source of such stories. It began to appear that the Utes were reponsible for most of the crime in the territory, even though the gold camps were filled with drifters, prospectors, and many less than desirable characters from the overcrowded eastern cities. The Utes were accused of setting vast numbers of forest fires in western Colorado. The rarely reported truth was that most of the fires were caused by lightning and by careless railroad builders and prospectors. Numerous other fires were actually set by settlers themselves to provide charcoal and to clear the land for grazing. One such man-set fire devastated thousands of acres near Aspen, Colorado, and actually leaped the wide Roaring Fork Valley borne on strong winds. Newspaper reporter Vickers' irresponsible articles even suggested that teaching the Utes to farm only created competition for arriving homesteaders and should be stopped. Occasionally, the angry Utes did set fires in an attempt to drive away illegal settlers, but this was a rare occurrence. The campaign of hate spearheaded by William Vickers and others kept newly arriving immigrants to Colorado in a constant state of fear of their Ute neighbors.

In a final crescendo of venomous yellow journalism, Vickers wrote that the Utes "are actually practicing communists" and "the government should be ashamed to encourage them in their idleness and wanton waste of property." Attorney, Frederic Pitkin, a lucky prospector in the Silverton area and soon-to-be governor, was an early leader in the drive to rid Colorado of the "ignorant" Utes. Pitkin encouraged Vickers in his vociferous anti-Indian tirades and soon appointed the editor to be his private secretary. Pitkin applied pressure as quickly as he dared, in defiance of the Bureau of Indian Affairs, in his campaign to force the government to move all Indians out of the state. Although practical in recognizing the incompatibility of the Indians' life-style with the growing state of Colorado, Pitkin in agreement with many voters placed no value on the rights of these first Americans. Like many of his contemporaries, he still felt that Indians were childlike and slightly less than human. They therefore deserved slightly less than human considerations.

An interesting sidelight showing an early tourist's opinion of Indian life was recorded in 1874. Richards and Company, a Denver firm, published probably the first tourist's guide to Colorado. The little book *Summering in Colorado* is a fascinating invitation to visit wild frontier country that had not been fully explored. The dangers of traveling in the wilderness are not mentioned, of course, nor is the lack of roads, hotels, food, or the occasionally fatal Indian dispute. More important matters are covered in glowing detail such as the salubrious climate, the invigorating hot springs, and the dramatic scenery.

The travel editors tell of traveling 300 miles west from Pueblo by light carriage. They visited Fort Garland and crossed Cochetopa Pass to the Ute agency at Los Pinos. There, the incongruous party of travel agents report on the Utes. "The Indians are queer specimens of humanity . . . they admire your blankets . . . beg for sugar . . . ride fearlessly, shoot skillfully, dress outrageously, live dirtily, and negotiate with visitors diplomatically." The authors also record various observations of reservation life, including the day-long lament of a woman whose husband had died. "She cut off her hair and had his horses and dog shot." They also remembered Chief Ouray leaving on an inspection trip of the reservation lands with his wife Chipeta. "They were driven in a two-horse Barouche with a driver. Ouray carried a long spyglass with him," the book reports. The carriage had been given to Ouray by the Colorado territorial government.

Ute freedom of movement was again being compressed from all sides. The mountain hunting lands were producing less and less game due partly to the wholesale slaughter by meat hunters who supplied the gold camps. About this time one group of illegal prospectors tells of rounding a bend on the Roaring Fork River and of coming upon a small group of Ute teepees set up at their regularly visited summer hunting camp. Their venerable leader, Washington, approached with his hand raised in the sign of peace. The old Ute pulled out a card that had been made for him in Denver, bearing his name and the message "This is a good Indian."

Despite increasing difficulties, the firm leadership of Ouray and his allied chiefs managed to maintain the peace. By calm reason and persuasion, plus occasional threats, he was able to keep his people's anger under control. The number of fatal incidents between the Utes and white invaders was amazingly small. By far, the majority of provocations, including an occasional senseless murder, were committed by the invading settlers.

Clearly, the anti-Indian group of politicians and journalists needed only one more confrontation to raise public sentiment to the point where the Utes could be driven away from their shining mountains. Finally in 1879, the necessary incident occurred that gave the anti-Indian faction their long-awaited opportunity. The incident is popularly known as the Meeker Massacre, and Meeker, Colorado was so named to commemorate the event.

Historical accuracy and fairness suggests that the affair should properly be known as the Thornburgh battle or the Battle of Milk Creek. The killing of Nathan Meeker was simply incidental to previous events, and the importance of the killing lies in the fact that it dramatically ended over 200 years of efforts by the Utes to coexist peacefully with the white man. Most importantly, this single episode ended many hundreds of years of Ute sovereignty in western Colorado.

Chief Ouray, *center*, with Shavano, Guero, Ankatosh, and Wa-rets of the Tabeguache (Uncompahgre) Ute band.

Severo, a tribal leader. His hair is braided with fur strips. The pipe bag is beaded and banded with quill work.

Chief Sapiah (Buckskin Charlie) in a popular hair and pipe bone breastplate. These were worn mainly for ceremonial purposes.

Chief Piah, *second from left*, with northern Utes. Note the different styles of buckskin leggings.

Nathan C. Meeker, reporter, poet, friend of Horace Greeley and Indian agent to the White River Utes. He died with a stake driven through his mouth.

MEEKER'S MURDER AND THE
THORNBURGH BATTLE

Traditional Ute luck suffered its most serious and fatal setback on a sunny September afternoon in 1879 during a rather bizarre affair that occurred quite by accident.

Nathan Cook Meeker, an ex-poet and newspaper man from New York, had recently been appointed agent for the White River Indian Agency in a remote section of northwestern Colorado. He was one of many political appointees sent west to administer the Indians, without training or knowledge of Indian culture. In fairness, Meeker was better qualified than some. But too many appointments were made due to pressure from friends in government or friends among the more active missionary groups.

Meeker had been a successful newspaper reporter and had written for Horace Greeley's *New York Daily Tribune*. The two men had become friends and Meeker had been partially responsible for Greeley's keen interest in the development of the West. With encouragement from Meeker, Greeley raised $100,000 by subscription to launch a land development scheme selling inexpensive farmland in northeastern Colorado. Greeley's subscribers were led west by wagon train to settle land and establish the much-publicized Union Colony, now Greeley, Colorado. Unfortunately, Nathan Meeker was appointed director of the group.

Soon after reaching Colorado, the settlers discovered that Meeker, although a good speaker, lacked agricultural experience and worse, was a most incompetent manager. Land that had been only recently advertised for sale at 90 cents per acre had been carelessly purchased by

Meeker from promoters for up to $5.00 per acre. Soon thereafter, a vote was taken by the indignant colonists, and the bungling Meeker was dismissed as director of Union Colony.

Heavily in debt and in his sixties, Meeker managed through friends to obtain an appointment as director of the White River Ute Agency. He desperately wanted to succeed in this new crusade in order to vindicate his reputation, which seems to have had as many failures as successes. If his knowledge of farming was sketchy, his knowledge of Indians' welfare needs was nonexistent.

During his earlier career as a reporter, Meeker had visited the West and once editorialized on the subject of "the mental inferiority of the American Indian." Meeker's principal mission to the Utes seems to have been teaching the Christian work ethic which, it was reasoned by many, would lead the Indians to embrace an agricultural way of life.

Farming had become the main thrust of the Department of the Interior's reservation programs for civilizing the Indians. In spite of well-meaning theory, the adoption of agriculture by the Indians met with great resistance and had relatively little success throughout the West. The northern Utes who lived on the White River had no tradition and little experience in farming. The Weeminuche Utes had once farmed in a very limited way. A few southern Utes had become skilled sheepherders, and cattle raising was beginning to gain minor acceptance in the southern part of Ute territory. But the transition from a hunting society to a materialistic culture and the acceptance of the difficult task of cultivating crops would take many, many generations. Even today, many Indian groups steadfastly refuse to farm. The northern Utes, Nathan Meeker's charges at the White River Agency, were among the last to adopt the different life-style demanded by western civilization.

In the late 1870s several traders operated new general stores in northwestern Colorado close to the White River Agency. Big Bill Morgan's store was situated west of Craig, and Charlie Perkin's trading post was located on the Snake River. The traders were eager to barter finely cured Ute deerskin for supplies and sometimes whiskey. The rate of exchange generally required a good Ute pony to buy a fairly new gun. This barter system adequately supplied the few items the Utes needed from civilization and further discouraged the idea of farming.

Nathan Meeker plunged enthusiastically into his new responsibilities at White River, convinced that he could control the unruly nothern clans and persuade them to accept the hard work required to farm the land. First, he diligently attempted to get the Indians to address him as Father Meeker. Next, Meeker found better and less rock-filled farmland four miles downstream from the existing agency location and unilaterally decided the entire agency should be moved there. The new location did have rich river-bottom land that had been used by the Utes to graze their beloved horses. Douglas and his followers reluctantly agreed to move to the new agency site. But the move caused dissension, and some Utes split into a separate group when Jack (Nicaagat) and Antelope, the son of old chief Nevava, refused to move away from the original agency location.

In the spring of 1879, Agent Meeker applied pressure on the aging Quinkent (Douglas) and his followers to plant a new field of garden crops. In order to force the Indians to plant, Meeker refused to release much-needed treaty supplies to the hungry Indians until the work was done. Later, to prohibit the men from leaving on their annual summer hunt, he required each family including the men to appear weekly at the agency in order to receive their allotments of treaty goods.

Douglas, a Yampa Ute, had failed to change with the volatile times and had lost much of his influence with his clan to the younger Nicaagat (Jack), a half-Apache who briefly lived among white settlers and had learned some of their strange skills. Douglas was approaching 60 and wore a distinctive, long, graying mustache. He was a wealthy man by Ute standards because he could count over 100 horses among his possessions and he was an avid horse racer and trader. Douglas more than any other northern Ute leader had tried hard to cooperate with the agency staff.

Fear and anger was continuing to build throughout Indian territory because of the increasing danger of confrontation between the Utes and the infringing settlers. A young Indian named Tabernash was murdered on a Grand County ranch for merely trespassing on property that his tribe had traditionally owned for centuries. Soon thereafter, a settler out cutting wood for his stove near Kremmling, Colorado, was shot and killed, apparently in retaliation for the Tabernash murder. There were other less fatal incidents being reported with increasing regularity.

In Denver, the imaginative writer William Vickers had recently written a new series of inflammatory articles concerning Nathan Meeker's troubles with the Utes based on information supplied by Meeker himself. Repeating words such as "savages," "lazy," and "the

Utes must go," he and other journalists were slowly arousing serious public indignation against the Utes. News of these unfair and often untrue articles were reported to Nicaagat by a friendly Indian trader. Among Vickers' most dangerous charges had been one claiming that the Utes had burned down the cabin home of a former Indian agent named Thompson. Knowing the report to be untrue and that in fact the cabin was still standing, Nicaagat made a long trip to Denver from the Indian encampments at White River. After much waiting, he was finally allowed a short interview with Governor Pitkin. Nicaagat recited certain Ute grievances to the governor concerning recent violations of the latest treaty. He also referred to the falsely reported Thompson affair and to many baseless rumors being circulated partly by Agent Meeker himself. As a representative of the tribal elders he also requested the appointment of a new agent for the White River Agency. Meeker, he said, was not running the agency fairly according to the treaty agreement and appeared not even to like the Indians. The anti-Indian governor attempted to be polite but nothing was done and the attacks in the press continued.

Canalla (Johnson) was a proud and controversial medicine man and a half-breed Ute who lived close to the White River Agency. He, like Douglas, was wealthy by Indian standards and owned a large herd of over 100 horses, which were his greatest pride. He often raced against horses owned by the southern Ute bands at the well-visited race track at Powell Park. According to Agent Meeker, the Utes' preoccupation with their horses had been the principal reason for their refusal to learn to farm.

Shortly before rebuilding the agency at the new down-river site, Meeker, ignoring all protests, ordered the grassy horse pasture to be plowed, in preparation for planting. Canalla, who used the big pasture for his many horses, was furious and confronted Meeker in his office. A stubborn man, Meeker would not be dissuaded from his plan and angrily told Canalla that he owned too many horses and should get rid of them. Seething with fury, Canalla grabbed Meeker by the coat and pushed him against the office wall. He then shoved the startled agent through the open door of the building, knocking him to the ground. Hearing the commotion, agency employees rushed to Meeker's aid as Canalla stalked off.

This incident seems to have destroyed Nathan Meeker's confidence in his ability to lead the Utes and introduced to him the prospect of

Canalla (Johnson), the medicine man partially blamed for the Meeker incident. The Indian scalps were probably given to him by the photographer.

another failed career. Instead of calmly assessing the volatile yet manageable situation and calmly formulating a peaceful solution, Meeker hastily composed telegrams to Governor Pitkin in Denver 200 miles east of White River and to the Bureau of Indian Affairs relating the incident with angry indignation. He urgently requested that troops be sent as soon as possible to support the agency personnel. "I have been assaulted by the leading chief, Johnson, forced out of my house and injured badly. It is now revealed that it is Johnson who has originated all the trouble here. His son shot at the plowman, and the opposition to plowing is wide. Plowing stops; life of self, family and employees not safe, want protection immediately, have asked Governor Pitkin to confer with General Pope."

By previous agreement with the Indians, the governor had promised that no military contingent would ever be allowed to enter the agency lands. But by 1879, the Indian wars had practically ended and there was little for frontier troops to do with their time. This piece of news from Indian territory appeared to be a good opportunity to give the bored troopers some field experience, so the army enthusiastically overreacted.

Quickly, two companies of the 5th Cavalry and one mounted infantry contingent totaling about 150 men were dispatched from Fort Steele near Rawlins, Wyoming, under the command of a capable officer and West Point graduate, Major T. T. Thornburgh. Specific orders were issued to the major that the Utes were not to be molested but that the presence of the troops could serve as a sufficient deterrent against violence. Therefore, the major anticipated a peaceful maneuver with pleasant bivouacs and good elk hunting in the beautiful autumn weather. The soldiers were accompanied by about 25 civilians who were eager to take part in this Indian adventure.

Several local traders encountered the troops inside the Colorado border during the march south. One of the traders immediately sent word to his Indian friends, warning them of the approaching military force. Unwilling to believe what he had heard, Nicaagat with a small group of Indians rode swiftly northward to see for themselves whether the dangerous report was true. Nicaagat (Jack) had been raised by a Mormon family in Utah and had served as a special scout for General Crook during the Sioux wars. He was still a fairly young man and spoke understandable English. As Nicaagat approached Thornburgh's marching column on his pony he asked to see the major. "Where you go?" he asked simply. After being told that the force was proceeding to White River, the Indians seemed to show little emotion and soon left. But that evening Nicaagat appeared again at the soldiers' encampment and again asked to confer with the major. This time in firm but calm terms he stated that the Utes did not want the soldiers to go to White River. He reminded the major that he would be violating treaty agreements with Governor Pitkin and would soon be trespassing on Ute territory.

Offering a compromise, Nicaagat suggested that five Utes and five soldiers should proceed to the agency to discuss grievances with Agent Meeker personally. Major Thornburgh considered the proposal and in so doing conferred with his own scouts. The scouts advised Thornburgh against making any agreement with the Indians and cited the possibility of treachery. Undoubtedly, in making his decision the major reasoned that the Utes were generally a peaceful tribe and had avoided conflict in the past where ever possible. No pitched battle of consequence had ever occurred between the U.S. Army and the Ute tribe except for a slight involvement after the so-called Christmas battle many years before. Many Utes had served successfully with the U.S. Army as scouts against their enemies among the Plains Indians. With these facts doubtless in mind the major decided to follow his original interpretation of his orders and proceed south in full force towards the White River agency. Nicaagat again left the army encampment.

The next day, about 15 miles north of the Indian agency lands, Thornburgh approached Milk Creek. His supply wagons had been lagging about two miles behind because of the rough terrain they were encountering. It was a sunny, sparkling fall day. But, unknown to the soldiers there was near panic in the Ute encampments close by. The Indians remembered the terrible story of the Sand Creek massacre of Black Kettle's band of Cheyenne. The tale had been told around many campfires of how 700 Colorado militia men under the murderous, Methodist preacher Colonel John Chivington had rushed down upon a camp of unarmed sleeping women and children. Black Kettle's Cheyenne had been camped in the proper place according to the government's own request. The men were away hunting buffalo and an American flag flew from Black Kettle's teepee. This did not stop the worst atrocity in Colorado history from occurring. At least 200 bewildered Indians were murdered, cut down with sabers, or shot while fleeing from their teepees. By actual count two-thirds of those killed were women and children. The remainder were mainly old men too feeble to accompany the younger men on the hunt.

Although it was 15 years since Sand Creek, the incident had never been forgotten by the western tribes, and now a fully armed force of uniformed soldiers was suddenly bearing down on the peaceful White River Ute encampment. Indian runners were sent out to attempt to purchase firearms from nearby traders. Some quickly took down their teepees and fled from the vicinity of the agency. Others moved their squaws and children to a new encampment on the far side of shallow little White River where it flowed past the agency.

During the previous night, Agent Meeker had discovered the young men performing a war dance and had tried to persuade Quinkent (Douglas) to stop the ceremony. But the normally cooperative leader simply shrugged his shoulders this time and walked away.

About midmorning the same day, Thornburgh's chief scout, Joe Rankin, with one soldier, was sent ahead of the advancing column to test the country and look for signs of Indians. Suddenly, a band of about 25 mounted men appeared on the bluffs above. Many wore the traditional yellow and black Ute war paint. Rankin raced back to Thornburgh's column to warn that narrow Coal Creek Canyon lay ahead, and conditions appeared conducive to the possibility of an ambush on the narrow trail.

Meanwhile, behind the hills, frightened, angry, and simply curious Indians were gathering from the surrounding countryside. Before long, 200 or 300 men had arrived, led by Nicaagat and Antelope. Most of the Indians were mounted, but many of the younger men were on foot, and only a few had modern rifles. Some had old and rusty flintlock muskets sold to them by the local traders in exchange for deerskin. Many of the younger men and boys had only bows and arrows or hatchets and clubs. A few were not armed at all.

Far to the south at the Los Pinos Agency, ailing Chief Ouray had left his comfortable house with members of his family to go on a hunting trip. He was completely unaware of the sudden change in Ute fortune about to occur at White River.

Little clouds of dust along the dry ridges of the nearly hills above Milk Creek revealed the presence of the Indians to Thornburgh's troops filing down the creekbed below. Thornburgh's wagon train still lagged behind. A few mounted Indians suddenly appeared over the ridge. They galloped their sturdy ponies down the hill and dashed across the creek between the troops and the approaching wagon train, to demonstrate their fearlessness. Major Thornburgh found himself threatened with being cut off from his supplies and in danger of being stopped or bottled up in the canyon ahead. Remembering his strict orders not to fight unless forced to do so, he allowed his advance troopers to deploy ahead in a defensive pattern.

The Utes above and behind the hills were uncertain of their own intent. They had approached the soldiers hoping to frighten them into stopping their advance toward the agency. They still hoped for acceptance of Nicaagat's plan to send a small delegation forward. Quinkent, the older, more conservative leader, had refused to become involved in the warlike maneuvering of Nicaagat's group and had remained with his followers at the agency.

Suddenly, in the confusion of nervous soldiers and excited, milling Indians, a shot was fired. Immediately return volleys from both sides echoed through the canyon. Breaking his orders out of necessity, Thornburgh allowed his troops to open a general barrage of return fire. He then personally led 20 cavalrymen, at a canter, back to support the isolated wagon train which by then was drawing into a defensive circle. Thornburgh hoped first to show the strength of his force and then negotiate a truce with the surrounding Utes. But before the troopers were able to reach the wagon train, the major fell from his horse, struck down by a bullet in the head. His horse fell with him mortally wounded. Major Thornburgh died soon, near the banks of Milk Creek. The stunned troopers, now under the command of a wounded Captain Payne, rallied on a low plateau beside the creek. Barricades of animals and equipment were quickly erected and rifle pits were dug in the center of the makeshift position.

At the White River Agency it was a pleasant day with a touch of fall in the air. The quarrelsome Johnson had earlier been invited to join the Meeker family at lunch and had seemed friendlier than usual. Unknown to Nathan Meeker, as he finished his noon meal, Major Thornburgh's body lay bleeding near a rocky ledge above Milk Creek. His uniform had been torn by bullets where he lay still unclaimed by his men in the unseen battle only 15 miles away.

At White River it was 2 p.m. when rifle shots suddenly broke the afternoon silence and reverberated through the peaceful valley. The clubbed and dying body of Nathan Meeker was dragged by frightened Indians out of his agency office into the afternoon sun trailing a smear of blood. Someone drove a wooden stake that pinned his body to the ground. Nathan Meeker was finally to gain the recognition he had vainly sought all his life by becoming the victim of a good, gory story, which in his newspaper days might have been one of his own.

After dark, scout Rankin managed to slip away from the beseiged soldiers at Milk Creek to ride nearly 150 miles north to Rawlins, Wyoming, to obtain help. He made the trip in an astounding 27½ hours, changing horses only three times for a near-record endurance ride. A lengthy siege of the surrounded and outnumbered soldiers was kept up by the angry Indians for nearly a week. Meanwhile, 35 black relief troops from the 9th Cavalry arrived from Middle Park under the command of Captain F. S. Dodge. Black troopers were especially respected by the Indians, who referred to them as "buffalo soldiers" because of their tight curly hair. The fresh troops reinforced the beleaguered solders, but the seige went on. Almost all of Thornburgh's 200 horses and mules had been killed, and the stench in the vicinity of the fortified camp was almost unbearable. Finally, after six days, a bugle sounded from up the valley and a strong relief column approached, under the command of General Merritt. The Utes had scouted the arriving military force several hours earlier and had already disappeared into the hills. The Thornburgh Battle had taken the lives of 37 Utes according to the best estimates. Twelve or more soldiers had been killed and 43 were wounded. The statistics are conflicting as was usually the case in battles of the period. No accurate casualty count could be verified of the Indian dead.

Meanwhile, Chief Ouray was informed by runners, about the raging battle at Milk Creek. He immediately dispatched his brother-in-law, Sapawanero, to ride the long distance from near Los Pinos to Milk Creek with a demand that the northern Ute band stop fighting, but Sapawanero arrived too late.

At the silent White River Ute Agency all seven agency employees lay dead. They had been killed the first day of the Thornburgh attack and some lay near the mutilated body of Nathan Meeker rotting in the sun. Mutilation of the dead was not practiced by the Indians for the sake of cruelty, but by damaging the body, an enemy was kept from going to the Happy Hunting Ground in one piece. During the subsequent investigation into the Meeker Massacre, Colorow explained that the stake through Meeker's mouth had been necessary "to stop his infernal lying," on the way to the Spirit World.

After the killings at the agency, Arvilla Meeker, the wife of Nathan, her daughter Josephine, and a Mrs. Price and her two children, were placed on horses and carried away with the fleeing Utes. Within hours of the killings, the White River Agency lay deserted and in smoldering ruin. Douglas, accompanied by the white women and children, teepees, supplies, and agent Meeker's cash box, hastily retreated south towards the Grand River (Colorado River). The desperate group crossed near present DeBeque and retreated up Plateau Creek to the high, forested, ancestral hunting grounds on Grand Mesa. Later they were joined by Nicaagat's warriors, who brought stories of the great battle at Milk Creek.

News about the "Ute War" traveled by wireless throughout the West, and eventually reached the remotest trapper's cabin and prospector's camp. A new tent city of silver prospectors which had been set up only months earlier on the site of Aspen, Colorado, was quickly dismantled. All but a few brave souls fled east over Independence Pass to the safety of Leadville. Wild rumors reaching far-away Fort Lewis reported that Animas City (present-day Durango) had also been attacked by the Utes and the entire population brutally massacred. Later, when federal relief troops arrived at the peaceful little mining camp, the false rumor was finally dispelled.

Fortunately, there were cool heads at the Department of the Interior in Washington, D.C. Carl Schurz, the controversial secretary, had many times been accused of being too friendly with the Indians. He had advocated giving each Indian family a private farm of 160 acres in order to effectively and peacefully break up the tribal system, but the idea was considered too expensive and the Indians never showed particular interest in it. Carl Schurz was a Prussian exile and had become a leading Republican speaker against slavery during the Civil War period and became a close friend of Abraham Lincoln. He was a major-general during the Civil War, and understood better than most the wisdom of treating the Indians fairly.

Rather than dispatch a military force in pursuit of the fleeing band of White River Utes and their captives, a course which might have cost many lives, Secretary Schurz appointed General Charles Adams, the Utes' old friend, to negotiate peace. General Adams was notified by

Arvilla Meeker, wife of Nathan Meeker. At age 63, she was kidnapped by the fleeing White River band led by Douglas.

dispatch about his new assignment, and he journeyed immediately from the Los Pinos Agency with a delegation of Utes representing Chief Ouray. The peace party included Sapawanero, Ouray's brother-in-law, and other recognized elders of the tribe. Their first task was to locate the mutinous northern Ute band in the big wilderness area south of the Colorado River on Grand Mesa. Finally, a trail was picked up, and 23 days after the abduction of the hostages the fugitives' encampment was found in the deep woodlands. After considerable angry negotiation the hostages were released by the White River band to General Adams' party.

Shortly thereafter, a formal committee of inquiry was set up by the federal government to investigate the uprising at Meeker's agency and to quiet the anti-Indian sentiment building up in the frontier towns and in the local press. Chief Ouray became the main spokesman for the Indian point of view and defense. The hearings had to be delayed until the rebellious White River leaders could be brought to Denver and with difficulty forced to appear before the Board of Inquiry. During the proceedings Ouray argued that the Colorado Indian commissioners were predominately prejudiced against the Utes and that only in Washington, D.C., could his tribe obtain fair treatment. He made a strong defense of this point, and soon the hearings were temporarily suspended and subsequently were moved to the federal capital. At Washington, Ouray again argued with reasonableness and force that indirectly all the participants had been responsible for the uprising, including Agent Nathan Meeker and Major Thornburgh. He showed that those who had ordered a strong military force to be brought to the White River Agency against previous treaty agreements were as guilty as the Indians themselves.

Arvilla Meeker testified regarding remarks made to her during her captivity by Quinkent, who had said that no violence would have occurred at White River if Major Thornburgh had not violated the treaty by marching into Ute territory. Ironically, old Quinkent was the only Ute leader who was willing to admit to having taken an active part in the uprising. He was arrested and sent under guard to Fort Leavenworth, Kansas, where he was imprisoned. After about a year of confinement, he was released due to the government's failure to file specific charges. In reality Quinkent appears to have been the leader who made the greatest effort to cooperate with Agent Meeker's bungling administration. Chief Ouray's shrewd eloquence, along with the even-handed negotiating of

General Adams and the wise Indian-affairs policies of Secretary Carl Schurz, saved the northern Ute leaders from trial and possible hanging.

Arvilla Meeker and her daughter Josephine became renowned and perhaps a bit infamous as a result of their forced experiences while being held captive. Josephine later made an extended lecture tour that packed in customers as she gave a vivid personal account detailing her shocking captivity to audiences of Victorian ladies and gentlemen.

For the Ute people spread throughout western Colorado, the Meeker affair was to be the final disaster in their long struggle for freedom. Even though it involved only a small band of relatively backward northern Utes, it was to permanently affect the entire tribe. Governor Pitkin and his anti-Indian faction of politicians and newspaper editors took advantage of a brief period of panic among settlers that followed the uprising to "rid the state of the Ute manace." But the governor was not able to fulfill the threat once made in the Denver papers that "unless the Utes can be removed from Colorado, they must be exterminated."

Nonetheless, following 1879, these proud people would never again be free to roam their beautiful high country as the undisputed possessors of the shining mountains and the blue skies. They were one of the last American tribes to pass under government control.

RESERVATIONS AND "UTE INVASION"

If history had decreed that the White River insurrection did not occur, the Ute people still could not long have coexisted as a free people with the swelling population of Colorado. If the inevitable solution had been delayed longer, the effect on the Utes could have been far worse, perhaps resulting in their complete destruction as a tribe.

Once again, just before he died, Ouray's wise, peaceful leadership had saved his tribe. The Utes could still accurately and proudly claim that they had never been decisively defeated by the white man's military force. The tribe was soon to make an honorable, although sad and difficult retreat to reservation land and much later received relatively generous cash settlements.

The following year, 1880, saw the final banishment of the Utes to their reservations. Ouray's Uncompahgre band (Tabeguaches) and the Yampa, White River, and Grand River Utes, all considered northern Ute bands, were ordered by the federal government to gather near Grand Junction, Colorado, in the spring. From there they were taken under heavy military escort on the long march into Utah. The gathering of the clans was accomplished with considerable difficulty because the people knew this was to be a trip of sorrow. The banished Utes were eventually resettled on a rather desolate section of the Uintah Reservation far east of Salt Lake City. The northern Utes were forced to leave their beloved mountains and valleys to live on the semi-desert plateaus and arid arroyos of northeastern Utah. Some are still there.

Two years earlier, by congressional legislation, all Utes remaining in northern New Mexico territory were ordered to move to the vicinity of the Los Pinos Agency in southern Colorado. The Indian agency that had

Ute hunting party fording the river near Los Pinos. Photo by H.S. Poley.

been operating at the land-grant town of Cimarron, New Mexico, was then closed. The formerly important old Indian agency at the little Spanish town and trading post of Abiquiu on the Chama River was also closed, thus ending over 200 years of historical Ute connections with the town.

The southern bands that were moved north out of New Mexico were mainly Mouache and Capotes, ancient Ute people whose ancestors had first made contact and traded with the Spanish in very early colonial times. These people were the descendants of the first Utes who learned to ride horses in the 1630s. By rough calculation, in 1875, the band had been greatly reduced in size, and only 350 Mouache Utes were reported living in the vicinity of Cimarron, their traditional home territory.

The removal of the southern Ute bands to Colorado was followed by the final treaty to be imposed upon Chief Ouray, and the only one signed under duress and without significant compromises. The Utes had no further opportunity to bargain after the investigation of the Thornburgh battle. The imposed agreement called for the removal of all northern Utes to the Utah reservation lands and further defined boundaries for the Southern Ute Reservation in Colorado. All other Indian territories were confiscated. Although there was very little room for negotiation, the leaders who signed the treaty at Washington, D.C., insisted that its terms must be ratified by tribal members after further negotiations held in Denver.

Appearing at these final meetings, a sickly Ouray represented the northern Utes while Ignacio, Buckskin Charlie, Severo, and Ojo Blanco represented the combined southern bands. The confirming agreement was later presented to additional elders and tribal members in Colorado by a five-member commission, which included Otto Mears, the Utes' friend and Colorado pioneer. The treaty of 1880 left no space to negotiate for territory. The agreement was simply read to the assembled Ute leaders and given to them to sign. Some refused, but nonetheless, the tribe was finally forced to begin a long painful readjustment to reservation life, an adjustment that still is debilitating to many Indians.

Chief Ouray did not accompany his northern bands to Utah. His health had been slowly deteriorating, and the attacks of nephritis increased. He became subject to moods of deep depression made more severe by the knowledge of the destruction of his lifelong effort to save his people from reservation life. Ouray said little about his health. He was now too sick to walk or ride long distances, so friends and relatives bore him on a litter to the hot springs for treatment. When Ouray realized his true condition during the last days, he left his adobe house at the Los Pinos Agency near Montrose to make a last visit to his friends, Buckskin Charlie and Chief Ignacio. His illness became worse and he spent his last days in his teepee near the town of Ignacio on the Southern Ute Reservation. When he died he was lying on a blanket wearing only the traditional loincloth. His painful death was attended by Chipeta, his wife, her brother, McCook, Buckskin Charlie, and many friends and army doctors. True to the Indian's inherent fear of death, Ouray was quickly buried in a cave on a remote mesa five miles south of Ignacio. The mouth of the cave was blocked with rocks, and five of Ouray's best horses were killed to follow him to the Happy Hunting Ground. Many years later, by government order, the body was disinterred, and Ouray was ceremoniously reburied at Ignacio, on the Southern Ute Reservation. Ouray died after insuring the ratification of the last treaty to be made by a free Ute nation.

The trip to Utah did not have a happy ending for the northern Utes. The Uintah Reservation had been created by executive order from President Abraham Lincoln in 1861. During the establishment of the reservation, the Indians began to realize that much of the land allotted to them was difficult, semi-desert country with very little wild game to hunt. The followers of Chief Black Hawk, originally members of the Salt Lake Ute band, had once refused to move to the new location. There followed a period of trouble known as the Black Hawk War, and the sporadic hostilities resulted in about 50 Mormon settlers being killed and many more uncounted Ute deaths. The principal result of this resistance was the erosion of Black Hawk's influence over the Utah Utes in favor of the more pragmatic and pliable Chief Tabby.

Some portions of the Uintah Reservation located in the Uintah River Valley do contain good farming and grazing land, but much of the area is dry uplands. Fortunately, an intelligent and conscientious agent was appointed to help get the reservation established; his name was J. J. Critchlow. During his tenure, farms and buildings were established, and slowly most of the Salt Lake Utes began to accept the Uintah area as their new home. However, the Indians always complained that the removal was unfair, and that essential hunting on their land was consistently poor. Meat had long been the mainstay of the Ute diet, and the bad hunting

Chief Sapiah (Buckskin Charlie) in eagle-feather headdress. He wears a Rutherford Hayes Indian Peace Medal and a traditional four-winds spiritual cross.

The trip of sorrow: in 1880, northern Ute bands were rounded up and driven from Colorado to the arid Uintah reservation in northeastern Utah.

forced the tribe to accept a government dole of cattle and flour.

The Uintah Reservation Headquarters was finally located at Fort Duchesne, about 140 miles east of Salt Lake City. By 1880, when the downhearted group of northern Utes arrived at the Uintah Reservation, there were many different groups of Indians living on the lands, and no one was pleased by the intrusion. Later, to lessen tensions, the Uncompahgre band was moved to a separate part of the reservation now known as the Ouray portion lying south of the Green River. The meager supply of game on the reservation continued to dwindle. To alleviate this perennial problem, the Utes were allowed to travel eastward each summer and fall to hunt on their traditional lands in the White River country and in the vicinity of Grand Mesa in Colorado. At first these small hunting parties were not interfered with. But increasingly, the Indians collided with settlers and travelers and frightened the ranchers and farmers who were rapidly moving into the former Indian territory. The settlers had been told that all Utes were permanently banished from north and central Colorado, and they were generally intolerant of the presence of these roving bands of Ute hunters.

In 1884, a group of cattlemen driving their herd to summer pasture near White River Canyon in the former northern Ute homeland were suddenly confronted by a band of armed hunters from the reservation in Utah. During the initial surprise and confusion, a cowboy impulsively shot and killed one of the Indian hunters who, he claimed, had stolen his horse. The enraged Ute party attacked the cattle drovers, but were easily driven off. Against their friends' advice, two reckless cowboys then pursued the retreating Indians into the nearby hills. Soon the two were cut off from their friends and were ambushed and killed by the Indians. As the Utes departed from the area, a voice, in clear English, shouted angry taunts at the embattled cowboys. He was identified as John Taylor, a black man, one of the many displaced black Americans who sometimes to escape slavery joined or married into various Indian tribes throughout the United States.

After Ouray died, the frequency of disputes increased briefly between white farmers, miners, and Utes. Most of the disputes were concerned with horse stealing on the part of the Indians and the increasing massacre of the game herds by the settlers. The stealing of horses and women between rival tribes had been an accepted form of warfare for centuries. In fact, the practice resembled sport more than war and was an important expression of machoism. Therefore, the theft of a few horses from the white man seemed to the Indians a small price to extract for the theft of their beautiful Rocky Mountain home, plus the near-complete decimation of their food supply and the curtailment of their right to hunt.

Personal belongings meant very little to the Indian, and by custom most property was owned by the women of the tribe. A little forced sharing on the part of the greedy miners and ranchers seemed natural in the context of Indian cultural values. Their social customs stressed the importance of generosity, and wealth was readily shared with friends and with other members of the band. Generosity was expected, and not sharing was considered very bad manners, if not a gross insult. Although the Indians did steal many horses from the white men, the reverse was also true, and on many occasions organized horse-stealing expeditions were undertaken by the arriving immigrants. Always wise in his dealings with the Caucasian Americans, Ouray recognized the dangers to his people of the repeated accusations of stealing. When Antelope, Nevava's son, was accused of appropriating a white man's horse near Florissant, Colorado, and reportedly had shot the man when he tried to take it back, Ouray promptly turned the young tribesman over to local authorities for trial. Ouray then saw to it that the tribesman received a fair hearing. Antelope was acquitted for lack of evidence.

Another more serious incident occurred in the spring of 1881 in Montezuma County near the Utah border. A posse of men had been organized to pursue and punish a Ute hunting party accused of stealing horses in the region. The group of settlers and ranchers set out in hot pursuit, as if on a holiday, eager for an adventure among the vanishing wild Indians. Foolishly, they followed the band into a narrow, rock arroyo, where they suddenly found themselves trapped. During the ensuing exchange of gunfire, nine members of the inexperienced posse were reported to have been killed by the well-positioned Indians.

Indian losses were difficult to determine and were not recorded after many skirmishes. The death of an Indian was not important news during frontier days. The Indians usually carried off their dead for proper burial, thus their losses were often exaggerated or inaccurately reported. Trouble was sometimes deliberately provoked by bored or drunken cowboys and miners looking for adventure with an Indian people whose ability to resist was rapidly fading into history. Such a situation occurred

Curious Utes were on exhibit themselves at the Denver Exposition of 1882. Photo by W.H. Jackson.

Winter was hard on the Ute reservations. There were frequent shortages of game and other food supplies.

in 1885, when a small group of southern Utes obtained permission to leave their reservation on a spring hunting expedition to replenish seriously depleted meat stocks. The hunting party was camped peacefully with their families on Beaver Creek near the present town of McPhee in Montezuma County, Colorado. At dawn, without warning or provocation, the little encampment was attacked by a group of drunken cattlemen and drifters. More than 10 of the surprised Utes were slaughtered, including a young father, who ran from his teepee clutching his baby son. He held the child high in his outstretched arms to show the attackers that the camp was friendly and included women and children.

Word of this especially vicious and unprovoked massacre spread quickly to settlers along the Dolores River, who expected quick reprisals. It was too late for the Genthner Family, who one night were awakened by the fury of flames engulfing their cabin. While trying to extinguish the blaze, settler Genthner was killed and his wife was seriously wounded by a vengeful band of Utes. In this case, perhaps for the first time, a serious effort was made to identify the cowboys who had created the trouble. Although no one was brought to trial, it was evident the West was slowly becoming civilized.

One of the last recorded Ute scares occurred in August, 1887. For the last time, the frontier press was able to sell newspapers with the inflaming headline "Ute War." The usual small groups of Utes had left the Uintah Reservation for their annual fall hunt and had been seen at several locations in the vicinity of Meeker. Reportedly, one Indian, probably drunk, had threatened a citizen he encountered on the trail. Memories of the "bloody Meeker Massacre" eight years earlier were quickly revived. Soon rumors of sightings of armed Indian bands were multiplied and circulated throughout the countryside. According to the newspapers, the hills were seemingly filled with bloodthirsty Indians. The mayor of Meeker, perhaps sensing a little free publicity for the town, called upon Governor Alva Adams for urgent military assistance. Hysterical stories of an invading Indian army prepared to retake their homeland soon created a general panic in the back country of western Colorado. Newspaper headlines screamed "Ute invasion." Eager volunteer companies of unemployed adventurers were hastily assembled at Aspen, Leadville, and as far away as Denver.

Amid patriotic fanfare, a sizeable posse calling themselves militia assembled at the prosperous silver mining town of Aspen. The heavily armed "heroes" rode out of town amid cheers from a large crowd of wellwishers. Aspen headlines bugled "Indian War," "Sheriff Hooper at the front . . . Pitkin County men help exterminate old Colorow and his band." As the enthusiastic mob approached Glenwood Springs, a local brass band played march music. Going through town, the posse was reinforced by eager volunteers from the local Glenwood bars. Other contingents marched from nearby settlements and mining camps. Eventually the armed adventurers gathered at Meeker, where the general stores did a booming business. An enormous amount of whiskey was consumed while the little army waited for action to begin. About a week later there had been no sign of war, and the militia men began to wander home disappointed at being cheated out of a real battle.

Actually, a very small posse did run into an even smaller Ute hunting party carrying a heavy load of recently butchered vension and hides, near Rangely, Colorado. A few shots were fired and during the brief exchange Sheriff Jack Ward fell dead and Frank Folsom from Aspen was hit and later died of his wounds. Again, in this unnecessary skirmish the Ute casualties were not considered important enought to be recorded. The Indian hunters quickly fled into the hills and soon returned to the safety of the Uintah Reservation in Utah. The following week Governor Adams of Colorado officially announced that the Indian War was over.

During the last quarter of the nineteenth century, almost all remaining free-roaming tribal Indians in the western United States were confined to reservations. After several decades some were certified as ready to enter outside society and were absorbed into western civilization, but many others were unable or unwilling to make the transition. The whole world was changing at a breathtaking pace. During this period it had become unofficial government policy to attempt to destroy tribal society and to coerce the Indians into accepting the white man's life-style by any means necessary. Eventually there was an attempt to modify and humanize these harsh objectives.

"GOD DAMN A POTATO"

Between 1880 and 1885 there was continuing political maneuvering between the state government at Denver and the federal Congress at Washington for the complete removal of all Utes from the Southern Ute Reservation in Colorado and resettlement on the Uintah Reservation. This would have left Colorado completely devoid of Indian reservations. Fortunately for the southern Utes, the people of Utah were equally determined that no more Indians would be settled in their state. On their own behalf, the Utah ranchers tried to lobby for the elimination of the Uintah Reservation so that the land could be sold or leased for cattle grazing.

At this time there was a new wave of reform regarding the administration of Indian Affairs and a belated awareness of the harsh treatment many tribes had received. Conscientious reformers such as Carl Schurz and General Charles Adams and a few others had fought for many years to obtain fair treatment for the western tribes. During the late eighties and nineties there could be heard a rising, guilt-ridden chorus of recrimination regarding the unfair and often inhuman treatment dealt the American Indians. This chorus had been heard before at times when there was no immediate need for Indians lands, but generally there was very little improvement in the treatment of the Indians over the centuries, and the same repressive methods of administering Indian Affairs generally continued in use.

Authoress Helen Hunt Jackson was among those who championed the Indians' cause. During speaking tours and in her sensational book *Century of Dishonor* she vividly described the killing and disgraceful treatment of the Indians. Her voice was joined by others, including former editor William Byers of the *Rocky Mountain News* and the influential and effective Senator Henry L. Dawes.

Senator Dawes of Massachusetts served for a time as chairman of the Senate Committee on Indian Affairs. He was a notably outspoken advocate of Indian rights and was responsible for major reforms in the Bureau of Indian Affairs. Senator Dawes effected passage of a landmark bill known as the Dawes Act of 1887. The law acknowledged, for the first time, the right of all Indians to become citizens of the United States. It also established the concept of individual land allotments or homesteads for the Indians and the rights of tribal land. This bill led to another Indian Affairs reform bill, the Hunter Act of 1895. The Hunter Act finally settled the southern Ute question forever and kept the tribe on their old reservation in southwestern Colorado. On an inspection trip of an Indian settlement in Oklahoma, Senator Dawes reported that he found no paupers, and that the tribe he visited owed no one, even though they owned their own schools. Yet, he said somewhat facetiously, "The defect in the system is apparent. They have got as far as they can go, because they own their land in common. Therefore, there is no selfishness which is at the bottom of civilization."

The Hunter Act, in addition to permanently settling the Ute reservation disputes, offered private farms to each tribal member as an individual allotment, usually a quarter section (160 acres) for a family and smaller plots for single invdividuals. Unfortunately, as an award to the anti-reservation faction, land not claimed personally could be sold to white settlers and ranchers. This accounts for the checkerboard pattern of many reservations and the many non-Indian-owned ranches and homesteads found within reservation boundaries today.

Chief Ignacio and a majority of his Weeminuche band refused to accept the individual family land allotments offered by the government. Ignacio feared such as system would break down close communal, tribal relationships. This, of course, was what the legislation was designed to do. The Weeminuches, who had very little desire to farm, preferred to continue their traditional communal society, living on common land shared by all. The 1895 legislation therefore provided a separate tract of land for the Weeminuches in the extreme western portion of the Southern Ute Reservation, in the heart of the Four Corners region close to Mesa Verde. The first Weeminuche agency was opened at Navajo Springs and later moved to Towaoc. This group has since been called the Ute Mountain Utes and is probably the most conservative of all the Ute bands. Another splinter group, separated from the Ute Mountain clan, had lived near Blanding, Utah for many generations. They refused to

Chief Ignacio, principal leader of the Weeminuches (Ute Mountain Utes) wearing a U.S. Cavalry hat and badge of the Ute reservation police.

move to the new reservation and have continued to live peacefully in the area just west of the Colorado border. The Mouache and Capote groups remain centered around Ignacio on the Colorado reservation and continued to be known as the southern Utes.

Farming was considered a loathesome way of life by most Plains and Woodland Indians. Although the govenment had spent sizeable sums of money and many years of patient propagandizing, by 1895 only a few Ute families had become full-time farmers. In 1891 there were estimated to be a mere 35 southern Ute families that had accepted farming as a full-time vocation. The southern Utes had for centuries observed Spanish farmers living and working the fertile valleys of northern New Mexico. Yet, despite this long exposure to the benefits of agriculture, the desire to learn strenuous modern-farming skills was almost totally lacking. For a second time the Bureau of Indian Affairs offered separate farm plots. Still many refused to accept because requirements for keeping the land included the necessity of farming the land. The majority opinion of the western Indians still seemed to echo the comment of Chief Washaka of the Shoshones when he said, "God Damn a Potato."

But slowly, sometimes imperceptably, changes were occurring. Under the leadership of Buckskin Charlie and Severo, more southern Utes accepted plots of land after observing their farming neighbors beginning to live better than they. Unfortunately, many of the private plots acquired by families were later sold legally to non-Indian farmers for cash. As a result, some families were again forced to accept government rations and support.

In 1899 under the terms of previous legislation, some unclaimed Southern Ute Reservation land was opened to white settlement, and proceeds from these land sales were added to the tribal treasury. Eventually the amount of Ute land sold reached 523,079 acres. Cattle and sheep raising had enjoyed a small acceptance by the tribe since very early colonial times and now increased faster than farming as one of the few alternative activities open to the Utes. Those who farmed or raised livestock began to live in government-built frame houses. Families still uncommitted to agriculture of any type continued to live in teepees or in mud-and-brush wikiups. They tried to hunt the diminishing supply of game, but many could not have survived were it not for the food stocks and other staple supplies doled out by the government in compliance with former treaty agreements. Rations given out at regular intervals kept many completely dependent families from starvation.

Severo, a Ute elder, and his family in 1889. The papoose boards caused wide, flat heads.

Today, there are some 298,000 tribal acres on the Southern Ute Reservation plus privately owned lands.

The Mountain Utes, largely Weeminuches, living just west of the Southern Ute Reservation, still own much of their land in common, about 553,000 acres. Much of it is arid plateau and semi-desert country unfit for farming. They assimilated very slowly into modern society until quite recently; currently, however, rapid change is taking place. The Ute Mountain people did not adopt their own constitution and set of written laws until 1940, while the southern Utes ratified a constitution and legal code almost a generation earlier, in 1926.

Very slowly the American nation has learned how to deal with the remnants of a once vast American Indian population. Ignorance and misunderstanding of Indian culture accompanied and corrupted U.S. government relations with the tribes for centuries. Yet, ironically, the government has been quite successful in coping with the immigration of millions of Europeans and Asians of diverse cultural backgrounds. As late as the 1870s and 1880s it was necessary for the U.S. government to commit about one-half of the field-ready troops of the entire United States Army in order to contain a tiny band of desperate Chiricahua Apaches led by the war chief Cochise and later by Geronimo. At the time, the Chiricahua's force numbered only about 340 warriors. The entire Apache "nation," according to a census of the time, included only 1414 men, of whom 1237 were listed as warriors, and 1851 women.

After the death of Ouray, Sapiah (Buckskin Charlie), a member of the Capote band, assumed the role of principal leader of the southern Utes. Like Ouray, he was part Apache. His father had been a medicine man and had been killed by the relatives of one of his patients. The sick man had died in spite of all prescribed treatment. Purportedly, Sapiah avenged his father's death by killing several members of the family responsible, but this was never verified. During his youth he took part in a fight with the Comanches, in which a bullet creased his skull and cut off his war bonnet. Buckskin Charlie, as he was generally called, led a long, colorful life, taking part in many skirmishes; he once served as a scout for the United States Army. He had been a long-time friend of Chief Ouray's and participated in several important treaty conferences with him. Sapiah accompanied Ute delegations to Washington, D.C., several times and had the distinction of marching in the inaugural parade of Theodore Roosevelt.

It was commonly understood that Sapiah would assume the leadership after the death of Ouray and the turnover of authority was generally popular. He continued to cooperate with the Bureau of Indian Affairs and reservation personnel throughout the remainder of his life. He valiantly attempted to persuade his people to accept the land allotments offered by the government and continually counselled them not to sell their land. At the same time, he steadfastly insisted on continuing many of the ancient tribal ceremonials and customs much to the annoyance of some government-appointed reformers. Sapiah also diligently encouraged the revival of the old Ute handcrafts, particularly beadwork and the expert tanning of deerskin. Ute craftsmanship had rapidly deteriorated following the peoples' confinement on the reservations and the subsequent breakdown of their traditional life-style. The Utes were traditionally skilled tanners, and Sapiah managed to create at least a small revival in the making of fine Ute buckskin products.

For public appearances, Sapiah usually wore fine buckskin clothing made by his people. He thoroughly enjoyed publicity and unlike most Indians was always willing to be photographed. Chief Buckskin Charlie lived a long and useful life. His death occurred in 1936 at the ripe age of 96. He chose to be buried in traditional Ute style, and a thin strip of ochre was painted from his hairline down over one eye to his chin. Interestingly, many pre-Columbian figures excavated from burial sites in Mexico and Central America, some dating from before the time of Christ, bear a similar thin stripe of ochre over the eye and across the cheek in symbolism of sickness or death.

Various experiments were tried during the early years of the 20th century to expedite the modernization process of the western American Indian tribes. Some of the experimentation proved to be more destructive than beneficial. Certainly, very little of the social experimentation designed to quickly prepare the Indians for western civilization was notably successful.

Despite the efforts of Buckskin Charlie and other leaders, handcrafts and many of the Ute ceremonies, rituals, and traditional folklore have been forgotten or modified. For a time, children were punished if caught speaking the beautiful Ute language in school. At the Indian schools at Fort Lewis and Grand Junction, Colorado, Ute boys were dressed up in military uniforms and given military haircuts. It was assumed that any In-

John Deal, Chief Buckskin Charlie wearing his Peace Medal, and Ocapoor encamped for a ceremonial in 1911.

Ute schoolchildren at the Indian School, Grand Junction, Colorado. The boys were forced to wear military uniforms, and only English could be spoken.

dian would make a good soldier because his ancestors had done so well fighting against the U.S. Army. This was not necessarily the case, of course, although there were numerous instances of Indian heroism during United States' involvement in foreign wars.

In retrospect American Indians were not nearly so warlike as their Christian-educated adversaries. In fact, when left alone, most tribes led notably peaceful lives. Yet, at least through World War II, myths concerning the natural fighting ability of the Indians were still reflected in government policies.

In 1912, the Utes were officially allowed to leave their reservations if they wished to do so. Many did leave and have since intermarried with other races and have been taken off the tribal rolls forever. In 1924, all American Indians automatically became United States citizens, perhaps one of the most superfluous occurrences in American history.

In 1931, distribution of rations to the Indians as a government allotment was finally terminated. The administration of welfare and relief for needy families was taken over by other agencies and in some cases was supervised by the tribe itself. Many Utes served their country well during World War II, bringing home stories of strange lands and cultures. During the 1950s, Ute children were finally transferred to regular public schools and Indian schools were closed. After a slow start, the attendance of Indians at public schools has increased rapidly during recent years.

The universal influence of television and its pictorial proof of the vast contrast between reservation life and outside American society has brought both dissatisfaction and new dreams and goals to Indian children as it has to other minorities.

The mean income of Ute families has steadily increased from a very low, near-poverty level a few years ago; but the average income for many families is still unacceptably low. In 1959, the combined tribe finally won a landmark lawsuit against the United States government. The suit, originally filed in 1939, claimed that large monetary compensation was due for tribal lands appropriated by the government and never compensated for under terms of the Treaty of 1880. After many years in court, a settlement of approximately $32,000,000 was made by the United States Court of Claims. Out of this, attorney's fees came to almost three million, but the substantial balance was divided among the Ute bands.

In 1961, in order to cut down on the number of Indian families still receiving government assistance and to cut down on the number of families living on tribal lands held in common, mixed-blood Utes, those with other tribal backgrounds or with less than one-half Indian blood, were asked to accept a property settlement ending their support to become absorbed into the general populace. As an inducement, they were given a lump-sum share of the Court of Claims settlement, and their lands were placed on the public tax rolls.

Today, generally, so-called full bloods live on tribal reservation land. The long but successful court suit filed for the Utes was very much the result of work done by Samuel Burch, then chairman of the Southern Ute Council, by vice-chairman John Baker, and their committees. A rehabilitation plan written by the staffs of these men is considered to be a model for modern Indian affairs. Recently, a renewed battle has been joined by the Utes in an effort to protect their legal rights to the diminishing uncommitted water supply in the Southwest. The complex issues may take years to resolve and the final decisions reached in various water courts will be far more important to the tribe than the 1953 cash settlement for land claims. Currently, the Blue Sky People are also involved in the evaluation of immensely rich oil, gas, coal, and uranium properties known to exist within the boundaries of their reservation lands. All three reservations, the Southern, Ute Mountain, and Uintah Ouray, may contain enough valuable energy deposits to make the Utes a prosperous tribe for generations to come. Meanwhile, the increased revenues already coming in from these sources has improved their financial security and caused an increase in the number of Utes registered on the tribal rolls.

On all three Ute reservations, numerous community improvement programs are in effect, including youth camps, Headstart, teachers' aid, federally financed housing for the elderly, new zoning and land-use programs, and others.

Today, Southern Ute Headquarters is located at Ignacio, Colorado, elevation 6,400 feet. It is near the center of a reservation still approximately 15 miles wide by 73 miles long. The tribe is justly proud of its beautiful new Pino Nuche Motel—Ute owned and managed. The complex, includes a swimming pool, restaurant, cocktail lounge, and craft shop. There is a big new indoor rodeo ring that is used for both Indian and non-Indian events, and the Southern Ute quarterhorse racetrack located at Ignacio is kept freshly painted and in good repair. Although it is still necessary to operate the Peaceful Spirit Alcoholism Center, the new HUD apartments are far more noticeable. There are approximately

New tribal administrative building, Uintah-Ouray Reservation, Fort Duchesne, Utah.

1000 Southern Utes registered on the tribal rolls at Ignacio. In the little cemetery of white crosses on the outskirts of town are names that bring back the not-too-distant past, such as Susan Wolf Bear, Antonio Buck, Jr., Clara Buffalo, Red Moon, and many others reminiscent of the days when clerks on the reservations sometimes gave the Indians new simple names to ease the problems of spelling.

Far to the north, the Uintah Reservation of eastern Utah is still head-quartered at Fort Duchesne. Like the southern reservation, it is checker-boarded due to land sales by nonfarming Indians at the turn of the century. There were also a few non-Indian-owned homesteads that existed in the area before the land was acquired for the Utes. These homesteads were exempted from Ute control.

The Uintah reservation combined with the Ouray portion shelters about 1,700 people on approximately 1.3 million acres. The original Utah Lake or Uintah band is centered around Fort Duchesne while the former White River, Yampa and Uncompahgre bands from Colorado were moved many years ago to their own separate portion of the reservation and their center is at Ouray, predominately semi-desert mesa country.

The old town of Fort Duchesne has not grown very much since early reservation days, and its development is overshadowed by nearby Roosevelt, Utah. It sits on arid high plains on a little bench of land by the Uintah River. Looking north during April you can see the snow on the peaks of the Uintah Mountains. While back and forth on nearby U.S. Highway 40, oil-field mechanics and engineers speed by, commuting between nearby Vernal and Roosevelt, Utah and the oil boom town of Rangely, Colorado, all centers for the vast new energy discoveries in the region. Some of the producing wells lie on Ute lands and already enrich the tribal treasury.

The Uintah-Ouray Reservation today looks forward to tremendously increased oil and gas revenues because the area is a part of the rapidly developing Overthrust Belt, probably the last large region of untapped oil reserves in the continental United States. Recently a suit has been filed in federal court in an attempt to expand the land area presently under Ute tribal control from the present reservation size of 1.3 million acres to its original outer boundary size of about 4 million acres.

Old Fort Duchesne was once a U.S. Cavalry outpost manned at one time by black troopers or "Buffalo Soldiers." The town later became famous as the sometime hangout of Butch Cassidy and his wild bunch of horse thieves and bandits. The old fort is gone, but the original Indian school where Indian children were forced to attend still stands on a hill to the north. On the main highway there is an attractive modern motel, Bottle Hollow Resort, which is operated by the tribe. It includes a restaurant, craft center, and attractive lounges. Next door in an oval building there is a small Ute tribal museum. The complex will become a part of Buffalo Run Dude Ranch Resort, with plans to offer horseback riding, fishing in a recently completed lake, craft exhibitions, and tours of the reservation and the nearby canyon lands.

A short distance behind the Bottle Hollow Resort buildings stands an impressively designed group of new buildings that contain the tribal offices and the Uintah community center. In addition to the resort, the tribe operates a tannery in an attempt to continue the Ute tradition of fine leather production. Ute Fab Inc., another tribal enterprise, turns out wood cabinets and fixtures, and the Ute Cattlemen's Association runs about 6,000 head of beef annually. Other enterprises have been attempted from time to time with mixed results.

At Fort Duchesne you can see the inevitable and necessary alcohol and drug abuse clinic. But nearby in the handsome, big, tribal gymnasium and recreation center, the Bear Runners are playing the Kicking Horse team from Montana as part of the annual basketball tournament. The cheerleaders are pretty, young Indian teenagers, carefully costumed in colorful dresses with wide beautifully beaded belts, beaded doeskin leggings, and elaborate ear pendants with round, beaded discs, a reminder that at one time the tribe was especially talented in bead work. Their long, lustrous black braided hair is dressed in fur wrappings. Each costume is different and mirrors family pride. Much of the fancy regalia closely resembles costumes worn by other western tribes, including both Plains people and the Pueblo groups. In recent years tribal costumes have tended to blend together among the western tribes with increasing similarity.

Ute parents are still experiencing problems in transmitting Ute traditions to the young people of the tribe. At the present time a tribal committee is attempting to promote increased usage of the Ute language inside the home, but due to a lack of interest among the young, the ancient Uto-Aztecean language is slowly dying. Truancy in the schools remains somewhat of a problem, but is far less wide spread than 20 years ago thanks to better motivation on the part of young Utes and also due in part to stricter rules regarding school attendance.

Generally, the Uintah-Ouray Reservation runs quietly as a small, fairly closeknit community of tribal members who are still proud to be Utes. There is increasing concern among all American tribes regarding the inactment of proposed legislation now being discussed in Washington. The new plan calls for radical changes in the control and administration of Indian reservations and according to some, threatens to destroy the reservation system. It may seem ironic that a system long hated by the Indians is now being defended by them as it is threatened with extinction. The reforms under discussion would transfer the management of all Indian reservations in the United States from the federal government to control by the various state governments where they exist. It is the feeling of many Indian leaders that passage of such a bill would be tantamount to desertion by the federal government and the Bureau of Indian Affairs. The resulting diversification of control, it is argued, would precede the complete breakdown of the reservation system and would mean the subsequent final death of what little is left of Indian culture. A change of policy of this magnitude would undoubtedly be especially difficult for the conservative Ute Mountain people.

The Ute Mountain Reservation is home to about 1,300 members of the Mountain Ute clan, not including the faction found in the independent Blanding, Utah, settlements. The Blanding Inidans are still settled peacefully in the Allen Canyon region of southeastern Utah where they lived long before their neighbors were confined to reservations. These remnants of the Weeminuche band who steadfastly refused to move to the reservation were supported in their stubborness by some of the white settlers in the area who helped pursuade the government not to interfere with their established homesteads. They were the only sizeable group of Utes allowed to remain outside the reservations after the confinement of 1880.

Recently, increasing income from gas leases on the Ute Mountain Reservation has indirectly led to dissension, and a few tribal members were accused several years ago of flagrant misuse of the tribe's revenues. It has been claimed that the increased wealth has filtered too slowly to its intended uses.

No one seems too concerned, however, and life goes on at a leisurely pace at the Ute Mountain Reservation center located at Towaoc. It is a small, pleasant town of neat houses clustered around an old army-style group of tribal buildings set around a rectangular mall. One of the old reservation buildings is the new Boy Scout headquarters. There is the Phillip Coyote Memorial Building, an old health center, a dining hall, and the administrative center. Across the mall is an attractive new health center and an impressive modern recreation hall and gym. Parked behind the buildings and anxiously awaiting the next racing season is a massive portable starting gate for the beloved tribal quarterhorse races. Racing rivalry between the various Ute bands is still keen, and horses remain the greatest popular obsession of some Indians, competing with the craving for automobiles and motorcycles. Down near the main highway stands a modern building dedicated to a new tribal enterprise, the manufacture of decorated and glazed pottery. Pottery making is not a traditional Ute craft, but this product is produced in traditional Indian designs and is attractive.

Sticking up incongruously in the almost treeless landscape outside town are new three- and four-bedroom split-level homes with carports attached, looking somewhat like the lonely sentinel buttes in the nearby desert. They may well be symbols of a dying heritage, obviously more comfortable than the drafty teepees and wikiups of a past age, but far less harmonious with the surrounding, unchanging terrain. There is the usual large population of contented dogs of obscure background still to be seen around the town; sleeping black and white bundles of fluff propped against almost every doorstep. Nearby, on a pile of dirt, an inquisitive gopher sits up brightly to survey the day. The little town of Towaoc seems to drift on without too much concern about or relationship with the changing twentieth century. Somehow this Ute Indian town seems in harmony with its rugged and rocky surroundings and with the blue, cloud-studded skies, and the brownish escarpments and tall canyon walls that fade into the distant desert. The Ute people, the town, and the immense expanse of nature around them seem at peace together.

Ute family with visitors in front of their wikiup which is covered with thick reeds and brush.

SPIRITUALISM, GHOST SHIRTS, & PEYOTE

Beginning on the day a Ute child was brought out of the birthing hut and continuing throughout his life, he was taught to live in close harmony with nature. Like all American Indian societies, the Utes lived with deep respect for the earth and the sky, the plants and animals, because understanding nature's lessons concerning the cycle of life meant survival.

All living things were considered to possess a spirit or soul and were respected as people of the universe. Only when necessary were plants harvested and animals killed. As Ute hunters and gatherers harvested food supplies, an apology was often murmured to the plant or animal being offended, such as "excuse me for taking this life, rabbit, but my family is hungry." Animals, too, went to the Happy Hunting Ground.

When an unfortunate tribesman became ill, he was considered to be out of tune with nature. This condition might have been caused by the patient's own mistakes or his bad living habits, or it might have been diagnosed by a wise medicine man as caused by an evil spell cast by an enemy. A medicine man was not called simply to cure the symptoms of sickness; it was his job to place the patient's lifeline spiritually back into harmony with nature.

Religion for the Utes was a totally personal experience. There was no complex ritual or formalized dogma, and certainly no regular priesthood or religious hierarchy. Religious experience for the Indian was spiritual and involved a very personal oneness with nature and one's self. Many gods were acknowledged and accepted by the Utes, but their form followed no single pattern. A god spirit might take on vague human form, while others were visualized in the form of animals. The physical appearance of a god, in itself, was not important. The most notable of the god spirits were generally common to all tribes, such as the spirit of thunder and lightning, and the spirits of war and peace and of flood. The blood god helped heal the sick. Indian gods explained the unexplainable as worship of a higher being or beings served all mankind.

Unlike many cultures, the Indians, and particularly the Utes, lacked a formal pantheon of spirits. Religion was simply a casual part of everyday life that was expected to explain natural phenomena and life itself. Most primitive cultures acknowledge gods very similar to those known to the Utes. But as other cultures became more sophisticated, major differences began to appear, created largely by the complexities of written language. In Greece, where mythology and religion had once been uncomplicated and certainly nature oriented, the use and storage of written records slowly created such an assembly of gods and complex religious dogma that it began to leave the people behind. Eventually, the increasingly rigid Greek pantheon of gods and religious requirements were crushed by their own weight.

Perhaps to the great benefit of their uncomplicated life-style, North American Indians did not develop written languages. Modifications in religious beliefs were rarely necessary for the Indian, because being based on unchanging nature, Indian religious worship reflected rather than conflicted with everyday life. Many stories and myths were based upon religious experience involving nature, and although they might vary slightly from tribe to tribe, their foundations were similar.

An important religious and spiritual experience occurred for young Ute men as they reached the age when they were ready to assume responsibility as an adult member of the tribe. As a youth approached maturity, he was expected to one day leave the village alone and travel to some remote and isolated spot. There, he would meditate at great length seeking a vision from the spirit world. This important message, when received, remained his talisman or guiding thought throughout his life.

According to legend handed down through countless centuries, the first Ute came up from a hole in the earth in order to view the green forests and the blue sky. He knew a supreme God, the Great Spirit, who lives in the sun. This God had many names, but they were not important, because he was God to all the people, bi-sexual and infinitely understanding. All Indians go to the Happy Hunting Ground in the sun after death to live forever with the spiritual God. Indian heaven is a good place like the earth, only better, with plenty of dancing and good hunting in the lush green forests.

The bear plays a special semi-magical role in Ute culture and is considered the second bravest of all the animals, exceeded in courage only by the fierce mountain lion. The Ute tribe still maintains a special friendship with bears, relating perhaps to their great love for the "shining mountains" where the bears live, and they once lived. Each spring this relationship is celebrated with a Bear Dance, and it is the most popular and most important of all the Ute dances. Although lacking in direct religious significance, the Bear Dance testifies to the spiritual connection between man, beasts, and all living things, and the intertwining of religion, legend, and storytelling.

Superstition still plays a part in everyday Ute life, as it does in many primitive societies, and some not so primitive. Superstitions learned from parents have served as useful teaching tools in the promotion of good social behavior and proper health habits since the beginning of civilization. Religion in its simpler sense serves the same purpose. Many superstitions teach obvious lessons. Others are not as obvious. The Utes believed that it is bad luck to allow dogs inside the house. Ghosts can cause illness that can only be cured by dancing or by a medicine man who understands ghosts. The wily badger possesses mystical powers that can cure foot trouble. Pituguf is a little green man who appears in people's dreams and possesses great power, both good and bad.

The shaman or medicine man was very important and enjoyed a sort of love-hate relationship with the tribe. He was expected to cure the sick, but also provided religious leadership in times of trouble. His mysterious songs usually appeared in a vision in his dreams and were taught to him by the gods. An unlucky or unwise medicine man ran great risks because he could be accused of inflicting bad spirits on his tribe or upon a single patient. If the evidence of his misdeeds was strong enough, he might be ordered killed by the elders of the tribe.

Strong belief in the hereafter is a cornerstone of religious experience for the Ute people, as it is for most tribes. As is true of many cultures, belief in a better life after death makes this life more bearable and gives meaning to otherwise unexplainable occurrences and a sometimes cruel fate. Very early in the Spanish colonial period, the Utes were exposed to the Christian church by the missionary padres in New Mexico, occasionally by force. Despite the diligent efforts of the

131

Catholic and later Protestant missionaries, Christianity had relatively little effect on them as long as their tribal society remained strong. The often-elaborate Christian rituals held little meaning for most North American Indians, and this new faith seemed to them extremely superficial. Christian spiritualism appears to have been too abstract to blend with the simple beliefs of a nomadic people who lacked all but the most sketchy record of their historical past.

With the passage of time, and the destruction of tribal society by western civilization, growing numbers of Utes have joined Christian churches, but sometimes they manage to introduce their own special variations to Christian ritual. The tribes that accepted Christianity most readily also tended to lose their own cultural heritage faster. The Utes began to forget their own past and customs simultaneously with receipt from the U.S. government of the free dole of supplies agreed to under various forced treaties. The loss of tribal culture accelerated rapidly during the early reservation period, after 1880.

Probably for the first time in Ute history, serious problems of rootlessness, depression, and general social unrest soon began to appear. As something tangible to cling to in a strange, new world, new cults often a mixture of Indian mysticism and Christianity emerged. Two important elements during this period of drastic change were the popular Ghost Dance society and later the Peyote ceremony, both of which caused a temporary spiritual awakening among the western tribes.

The much-discussed Ghost Dance swept like a whirlwind through many tribes in the southwest and the plains states, as the Indians mourned the death of their beloved way of life. The causes and the meaning of the Ghost Dance were misinterpreted by military authorities who controlled the tribes at the time, and they soon banned its performance. Yet, in spite of the ban, the dance became a last mania of hope and a final plea to the great God in the sun to rescue his friends, the Indian people, from the smothering and corrupting blanket of the white man's civilization.

The Ghost Dance was one of the most religious ceremonies of the late Indian period, and seemed to interplay a strange mixture of traditional Indian beliefs with Christianity. In 1870, Tavibo, a Piute Indian living on the Walker Reservation in Utah, went into the mountains and experienced a spiritual revelation. In his great vision he saw all mankind suddenly being swallowed into the earth. Then, after three days, only the Indians were returned to the surface of the earth, along with all the wild game, the fish, and all of nature, and they were destined to live forever without the white man. This was the age-old story of the end of the world and rebirth.

The mystic Tavibo died, but his son inherited his vision. Raised by a Mormon family of farmers in Utah, Wovoka, the son, was undoubtedly exposed to the Christian church, where Bible stories also told of visions and supernatural occurrences. In 1889, Wovoka retold of these visions at the first Ghost Dances held near Walker Lake. The message spread like a grass fire, and Wovoka soon became a great Indian evangelist and messiah. He preached the coming of a great, all-consuming flood and of the subsequent re-emergence of the ancient Indian ways as the dominant force in the world. A special magic Ghost shirt was worn by the faithful. Made of simple loose fitting white muslin or deerskin, this sacred blouse was decorated with spiritual symbols and was said to be impervious to the white man's bullets. Many Ute tribesmen joined the Ghost dancing at Walker Lake and elsewhere. Soon the popular dance cult was carried to the Kiowas, the Cheyennes, and Shoshones on their far-flung reservations. After learning of the Ghost Dance, Kicking Bear of the Sioux had a vision in which the white man's savior appeared, and he was in reality the Piute messiah, Wovoka. Kicking Bear carried his message to old Chief Sitting Bull of the Hunkpapa Sioux. By this time, many western tribes were gathering to dance the Ghost Dance and chant the Ghost Dance song,

> The whole world is coming
> A nation is coming   A nation is coming
> The eagle has brought the message to the tribe
> The father says so   The father says so
> Over the whole earth they are coming.

Wovoka delivered many speeches and argued that Christians must certainly be evil to have allowed the killing of their own savior, Jesus Christ.

Old Chief Sitting Bull was persuaded to come out of his retirement and endorse the new intertribal Ghost Society. In 1891, Yellow Nose, a Ute who had been held prisoner by the U.S. Army, recorded the story of the Ghost Dance for the first time in a beautiful pictograph illustration painted on deerskin.

Although apparently peaceful in its intent, the Ghost Dance and its strong rallying power for the Indians greatly disturbed government authorities. General Nelson Miles, commandant of the Military Department of the Missouri, became concerned that the new secret society

Ute in headdress made partially of eagle feathers.

might become the catalyst for a general Indian uprising, which might spread through all the western reservations. He therefore ordered that all Ghost Dancing should be stopped and all Ghost shirts confiscated. The ban was carried to all three Ute reservations, but resistance to the order was widespread among all the tribes, and it was carried out only with the greatest difficulty. Almost in desperation, the army ordered the arrest of Chief Sitting Bull to hold as a hostage to insure the termination of the Ghost Dance. Unfortunately, the old chief, a famous war leader who had once defeated General Custer at the Battle of Little Big Horn, was needlessly murdered by frightened Indian police, who had been sent to carry out his arrest. The sudden death of their respected leader panicked the Hunkpapa Sioux, who at the time of the murder were coming to join the Ghost Dance. Their pursuit by the army resulted in the inhuman and callous massacre of over 200 Sioux men, women, and children. At the time of the sudden attack, the tribe was peacefully encamped, low on food and largely unarmed, near the banks of now infamous Wounded Knee Creek in South Dakota.

Overreaction by the government and unnecessary killings followed by the violent suppression of the Ghost Dance dealt a final death blow to the faith of many Utes and other western Indians in their own culture. Wovoka, the Messiah, had preached nonviolence and a trust in God, and had promised his followers that the white man would disappear. Although wearing of the supposedly impervious Ghost shirt had been a late embellishment started by other leaders of the movement, it certainly did not repel army bullets. No Indian medicine was any longer strong enough to save the people.

In retrospect, the Ghost Dance Society, if properly managed, might have provided a bridge to draw Indian religion and the Indian people closer to an acceptance and understanding of western society. In fact, the harsh suppression of the movement caused many Indians to draw inward in utter despair and to further reject the ideas of the white man.

The outgrowth of this disruption, and the attendant breakdown in their will to survive as a people, caused some Indians, including some Utes, to turn towards even more exotic cults, the most popular example being the Peyote Ceremony. The use of peyote goes far back into Indian history. It was reported being used by the Spanish in the New World during the sixteenth century, and at that time its significance was totally nonreligious. Later, however, peyote began to be used both as part of the religious ceremony in Christian Indian churches, and also outside the church in remote parts of the reservations. Individual members of the Ute and other tribes have been attracted by the hallucinatory visions and spiritual experiences that the use of peyote can induce. The ceremony has been practiced by the Navajos, Bannocks, Utes, Sioux, Hopi, and many others. At one time, peyote became an integral part of religious ceremonies practiced by the Native American Church. As such, its use is now carefully restricted under laws adopted by the Navajo tribe.

The Peyote Ceremony usually takes place at the climax of a nightlong religious service, which includes Christian hymns, Indian chants, and continued prayer. The button of the peyote plant containing mescaline is revered in itself as a religious symbol by a few participants. During the ceremony, it is finally eaten by the celebrants and creates hallucinations, sometimes in vivid colors, and causes a loss of the sense of reality. This temporary euphoric uplifting experience has sometimes been abused and increasingly is used outside the church simply for its escapist qualities. The use of peyote, however, is not considered by health authorities to be particularly harmful nor habit forming. Although regulated under the Federal Pure Food and Drug Administration, its use for religious purposes has been legally approved as late as 1970 by the California Supreme Court in the landmark case, *People vs. Woody*. Today, peyote is grown mainly in Mexico.

Recently, there has been a concerted effort to encourage Indians to preserve whatever remains of their rapidly disappearing cultural heritage. Both the government and tribal leadership are attempting to rebuild knowledge of the past among Indian people. The task has been difficult for the Utes because so much of their culture has already been lost since the accelerated decline that began in 1880. Nonetheless, tribal leaders and many Ute parents attempt to teach their children to separate modern religious interpretations from the more direct spiritual values of their ancestors.

There is currently a grass-roots movement among many members of the tribe to preserve the melodious and ancient Uto-Aztecean language in the home, so that the children will become bilingual. But living with two languages and attempting to accommodate two different and diverse cultures become increasingly difficult in the television age.

HUSBAND ABUSE
AND BIRTHING HUTS

Utes, in conformity with the customs of most tribes, normally married during their teenage years. Typically, the young man about to be married was 18 or 19 years old and the girl, 14 or 15. Both courtship and marriage were simple and direct matters and there was little or no formal ceremony. After a certain amount of flirtation during which the boy made his intentions known, he would simply move in with the girl's family, if they agreed to accept him. Later, the young couple acquired a teepee or wikiup of their own and lived as a separate unit of the clan.

There was, however, a certain amount of loose protocol common to courtship that might take the following form. Having met an interested girl, perhaps during a winter visit between several families or clans, or perhaps during the spring Bear Dance, the boy might decide to take action. Hiding himself near the girl's teepee in a tree or bush, the young man would sing to her about his love and about his great bravery and strength. Sometimes he would serenade her with songs played on a wooden flute. Soon thereafter, the potential husband was expected to pay a visit to the girl's family, bringing gifts. During this visit it was customary for him to ignore the girl's presence, concentrating his attentions on the rest of the family. If the boy was not rebuffed by this time, both families would soon meet to discuss the details of the marriage. Another popular courting ritual was sometimes practiced by the Utes. A young suitor would go into the woods and kill a deer. At night he would hang the carcass on a tree branch near the girl's teepee. If she wished to accept her lover, she would skin and dress the animal, then build a fire

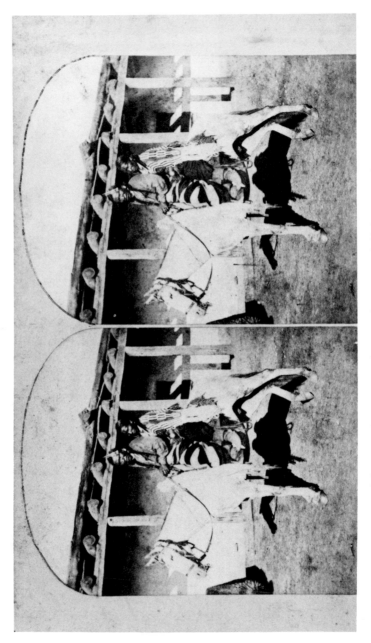

A Ute with his squaw. (From a stereo-dimentional viewing, probably by W.H. Jackson.

and prepare her future husband a meal. After the feast the marriage was consummated. One old custom of the southern Ute clan was called "smoking," and its purpose was to test the physical fitness of the bride and groom. The male or the female suitor was placed by the other party's family into a sealed teepee containing a very smoky fire. The suitor was left inside long enough to test his or her endurance and resistance to sickness.

Polygamy was known, but was not particularly widespread. Its popularity depended upon the need to provide shelter for surplus women of the tribe and upon the availability of captured Indian slaves. There was a great sense of responsibility to the clan, and a Ute man might marry two sisters, or a woman and her aunt, particularly if the aunt had raised and cared for the girl.

There was also an instinctive awareness of the need to mix blood in marriage, and as a result intercourse between close family members was rare, but marriage was quite common between members of different Ute bands. Over the years there were many marriages between Utes and their close friends the Jicarilla Apaches, and occasionally a Ute would take a neighboring Bannock or Snake woman for his bride. Marriage to women captured from enemy Plains tribes such as the Cheyenne and Arapahoe was also fairly frequent and allowed a valuable exchange of tribal customs and ideas.

During the seventeenth and eighteenth centuries this exchange of wives resulted in greatly improved living habits and customs and the Ute life-style became increasingly similar to the more advanced Plains Indians. Occasionally, the affections of a wife might be stolen by another man, causing the woman to leave her husband. The offended spouse was expected to retaliate, but he might or might not attack the offending man in what was considered a justifiable fight. By custom, the losing husband could elect not to fight but might decide to avenge his honor by appropriating or killing the best horse belonging to the other man. Such action was considered an honorable revenge for his wounded pride.

Divorce was tolerated in Ute society with an ease and understanding equal to the informal and casual marriage process. No papers were ever filed and no permission was necessary. The unhappy partner simply dissolved the marriage by gathering his clothes and moving out. This sometimes resulted in violent quarrels between two angry knife-wielding women, and husband abuse was not uncommon among the Indians, depending upon the wife's physical prowess. Indian women were almost as strong as men and could certainly not be considered the weaker sex; in fact, when sometimes there was a shortage of men, the women were trained to hunt and take part in battle. When a member of the tribe lost a mate through death or divorce, he or she was usually taken in by the family group and given food and shelter. As long as there was sufficent food, it was shared by all without reservation, but if food was scarce, the single person would be expected to leave the group.

Childbirth was a family affair, but the actual event occurred in the privacy of a birthing hut. The expectant mother built the hut separate from the main teepee and birth was given there, with the husband present until the beginning of labor. The mother and father lived together in the tiny hut for about 10 days before delivery. At the first signs of labor, the father would leave the hut and go for a long run up and down the nearest hill until he was exhausted. This ritual helped insure that the baby would be strong and a good runner. The father did not return to the hut after his long run, but returned to the main teepee and waited for his wife to join him with the new baby.

Ute infants spent most of their time strapped to cradle boards. Carried on their mother's backs during her daily chores, they were usually placid and happy children used to being a constant part of the camp life and family activity. Many Plains and Woodland Indians typically have broad, flattened facial features and a noticeably flat back portion of the head. This is partially due to the flattening of the skull caused by the hard cradle boards to which they were strapped. Ute children were rarely disciplined except if necessary to guard against certain dangers. They roamed freely about the camp and were accepted as an equal part of the family and as full members of the village community. They were taught by the whole tribe including special influence from the grandparents and village elders. Early trappers who explored the west noted in their diaries that Indian children rarely seemed to cry and generally seemed happy in their secure tribal environment.

Until the 1950s many Ute marriages were still being conducted in the informal manner by simple consent and cohabitation. Because divorce was accomplished by simple lack of consent, Indian society included many children who had one parent or no parents. There were other reasons for the large number of orphans, including a shorter life expectancy, war, and associated kidnapping. Under the tribal system, these children were well cared for by family groups within the tribal com-

Ute mother and child with papoose. The hide cradleboard has intricate quill work across the top.

munity, and there was no stigma connected with illegitimacy. However, with the rapid breakdown of tribal society in the early twentieth century, there was a serious increase in the problem of illegitimate and neglected children among most tribes. For a long time, the problem was acute due to the loss of communal responsibility and an increase in the birth rate. In recent years, however, marriage has more closely followed the pattern of U.S. society as a whole. Today, there are many more legal marriages among the Utes, and subsequently the number of children lacking parents is diminishing. The change seems to have come about due to community acceptance of the new customs more than from religious pressure.

The Ute Agency at Abiquiu, New Mexico, 1880, shortly before the Utes were transferred to the Southern Ute Reservation in Colorado.

NOT HUNTING FOR WAR

Hunting was the principal occupation of the Ute tribe and the most vital source of their food supply. The men had few responsibilities beyond hunting and the care of their horses, the defense of the village and warfare, and some spiritual observances. In early times men also helped in the preparation and tanning of deerskin, but they seem to have turned that task over to women after the tribe acquired horses and the men began to travel on extended buffalo hunts.

Women were responsible for almost all other domestic activities such as cooking, making clothes, and raising the children. Women were also expected to care for the packing and transportation of personal possessions and the erection of tents at each new campsite, and they sometimes even followed the men into battle.

Before 1640, the approximate date when horses were first obtained from the Spanish, hunting was done on foot with bows and arrows, lances, and crude knives. Before the development of the bow and arrow, early Colorado hunters used the atlatl, as the principal weapon for bringing down big game. The atlatl was a strange weapon, basically a lance which could be propelled by placing the butt end into the notch of a hand-held stick. The resulting fulcrum added great speed and distance to the thrust of the weapon. Lances with sharp stone points and stone axes predated both the bow and arrow and the atlatl by thousands of years. In fact the development of the bow and arrow is relatively recent. The first evidence of their use in North America appears about 500 A.D., and within a short time their greater power and accuracy had completely replaced the use of the atlatl. Big game, such as deer, elk, bear, and buffalo were tracked for many miles on foot by fleet-footed runners. The Indians could not outrun the animals, but they could often out-maneuver them; therefore, big-game hunting required carefully planned ambush and tedious stalking. Sometimes many grueling days of silent stalking would end without a successful kill and Indian families would experience serious food shortages. The great moving buffalo herds were often followed by Ute hunters from the far western slope of the Colorado Rocky Mountains as far as the front range west of Denver, a distance of several hundred miles. The huge beasts with their thick tough hide and great thundering speed were difficult to bring down, so the Indians attempted to stampede them over hidden cliffs or lure them into a blind canyon where hunters were waiting to make the kill.

Recently, evidence has been discovered revealing a unique method of hunting large grazing animals such as deer and elk long before the time of acquisition of horses. Near Trail Ridge Road on the northeastern slope of the Colorado Rockies, the remains of low stone walls have been found, originally perhaps one and a half to two feet in height. The walls ran at an angle to each other for a great distance becoming closer and finally converging in a wedge. Inside the narrow point of the angle a pit was dug, large enough to hold and conceal many well-armed hunters.

The quietly grazing animals were slowly maneuvered onto land between the low stone walls by other hunters or by squaws who followed them at a distance, sometimes dressed in animal skins themselves. Not sufficiently frightened enough to panic, the animals did not jump over the low stone walls, but unsuspectingly allowed the walls to guide them steadily into the point of the wedge. When the game had finally grazed close enough to the camouflaged pit, a flight of atlatl spears or arrows was loosed at them from both front and rear.

Hunting was of prime importance to the Utes, and to a great extent dictated their life-style. The better meat hunters they became, the stronger and healthier they became as a tribe. All of the Colorado high country was their semi-private hunting domain with only an occasional intrusion of short duration by the hated Arapahoes. Beautiful Middle Park, west of what is now Rocky Mountain National Park, and South Park, located in the high, dry lake basin above and west of Colorado Springs, were among the Utes' favorite hunting grounds. Here, vast herds of buffalo, elk, and deer roamed the grasslands, antelope and mountain sheep were usually abundant, and there were grizzly and black bear, and mountain lion. Small game abounded in the region such as grouse, ducks, geese, wild turkey, sage hens, and jack rabbits. There was rich grass and shelter from the winds in this beautiful high country, and not too far away were soothing hot springs in which to revitalize tired bodies. Only occasionally did the Plains Indians venture this far west in search of tent poles, buffalo, or salt. The Indian tribes of the plains were generally fearful of the tough Utes and superstitious about the dark forests and rugged mountains, which the Utes knew so well. The Cheyennes among nearby Plains tribes were considered less brave than the Arapahoes and very rarely ventured into dangerous Ute territory.

An early rancher named Samuel Hartsell, living at the edge of what was then called Bayou Salado, now South Park, recalled watching the aftermath of a fierce battle between a hunting party of Utes and a war band of Arapahoes and Cheyennes, who had both been stalking the same buffalo herd. Thinking the war band was a group of more friendly Utes, he allowed himself to be captured. He was shown Ute scalps and a captured Ute boy, trophies of the recent battle. Fortunately, after taking his gun and knife, he was released by the Arapahoes.

Love of war and combat was not widespread among the Indian tribes, contrary to what the makers of western films would have us believe. Although formidable foes when the occasion required, the Utes did not place high value on being great warriors. Although the tribe did go through short warlike periods, particularly after their acquisition of horses, war was generally considered a nuisance associated with territorial disputes and the consequence of the occasional need to acquire horses and women.

The Utes usually were a "lucky" tribe and certainly were fortunate to obtain horses 50 to 100 years earlier than most tribes. On the backs of their horses they could venture over wider territory in search of bigger game herds and soon found it easier to raid enemy encampments, whose inhabitants still hunted and fought on foot. Utes, mounted on the backs of the terrifying "magic dogs," could gallop swiftly into an enemy camp and carry off goods and captives before an adequate defense could be organized against them. Soon Spanish settlers on remote ranches and in mining camps in northern New Mexico reported being robbed and raided by bands of mountain "Utahs" on the backs of stolen Spanish Barb horses. At the territorial capital at Santa Fe, complaints concerning Ute raids increased until the first peace treaty was signed with the tribe. Later, in 1692, having persuaded the Utes to stop their occasional costly raids, thus relieving his weary troops, Don Diego de Vargas was finally able to establish a period of peace in northern New Mexico following the quelling of the disasterous Pueblo rebellion. The period of relative peace continued between the Utes and the Spanish settlements with only occasional hostility well into the 18th century.

The Utes occasionally became involved in minor territorial battles with rival Plains tribes during this period due to the uncertain migratory habits of the game herds.

The tough Navajos and the Indians of the pueblos were badly weakened by their long war with the Spanish, and along with the Comanches, occasionally became victims of raids by well-mounted Ute horsemen. Some of the more peaceful Pueblo Indian people located in remote areas north of Santa Fe were frequently victimized and raided for equipment and slaves. Ute attacks were sometimes encouraged by the Spanish, who bought the Indian captives brought to them by Ute raiding parties and then drove these unfortunate Indian slaves in chains to work in the shops and industries of the settlements and in the newly expanding mines.

Fine Navajo cottons, woolen goods, and Pueblo pottery could be acquired during raids and these items were coveted by women of the Ute tribe, who did not include weaving or pottery making among their best skills. Historically, women had been given the tedious task of following their men into war, but unlike the mounted warriors, the women travelled on foot. When loot was obtained from the enemy, it was the squaw's job to carry it home walking. Although horses were usually available, they were the most prized possession of the Ute tribe, and therefore considered too valuable for women to ride into enemy territory.

Indian warfare was rarely the scene of mass mayhem or bloodletting such as was traditional in European warfare of the time. Far more important than the death of an enemy was the capture of his horses, his women, and his other personal property. Life was sacred to the Indian and far too precious to risk unnecessarily. Most Indian warfare was launched by stealth, the element of surprise being all important because the conflict was not expected to last very long. Looking as ferocious as possible with their nude bodies painted in stripes of yellow and black war paint, the Utes would swoop down on an enemy camp, riding their best and most fleet-footed horses, screaming insults, and making fearsome noises. Quickly, the dashing warriors grabbed whatever loot was within easy reach including as many horses as possible, and then disappeared over the nearest ridge to safer ground, before too many enemy warriors had time to join in the fight. The death of two or three of the enemy was considered a satisfactory victory and at that point, both sides usually retreated to celebrate their victory with dances or to lament their defeat.

Occasionally if both sides mounted a considerable force and the outcome of the impending battle appeared to risk too many deaths on both sides, a truce might be called. A warrior might then be selected from each side to engage in single combat; the outcome would determine which tribe won the battle. The losing band was assessed a tribute of some sort payable in horses or weapons or squaws.

Counting coup in battle was considered very important by some tribes, but the practice never became popular among the Utes. A coup in battle meant wounding or sometimes merely touching the person of the enemy, or better still, grabbing a piece of his clothing or equipment. Such trophies were carried home proudly, and a warrior's collection of battle souvenirs was carried on his person or displayed in his teepee. The honor of making coups was recounted over many campfires and increased a warrior's prestige within the tribe.

The Utes were considered to be more or less at war with the Comanches during the first half of the eighteenth century, although this resulted in very little actual battle. The Arapahoes and Sioux were considered permanent enemies of the Utes, and there were periodic skirmishes between small bands representing these neighboring tribes. Scalping, although occasionally practiced by some early Indian societies, was also brought to the New World by the Spanish. This grisly ritual had been practiced in parts of Europe, where an enemy scalp might be required as proof of death in order to collect a bounty from the king.

There were many stories retold to succeeding generations of Indian children about the battle prowess of their ancestors. Some of these stories have been handed down for centuries and have survived to provide helpful clues in the monumental task of piecing together the threads of Indian history.

The following story was reported by a northern Ute to anthropologist Dr. Edward Napir. It illustrates the somewhat casual attitude of the Indians towards their enemies and the pursuit of war. "A little dog belonging to an enemy tribe wandered into the camp of a Ute hunting party many years ago. It was night time, and the Utes decided to trick the enemy. They built a campfire in the woods and tied the little dog close to it. Then they went away and hid in the dark of the forest. Soon the moon came up and the Utes could see the owner of the dog approaching. The Utes got their bows and arrows ready and quickly surrounded the enemy. A Ute warrior decided to avenge the death of a relative who had recently been slain by the enemy's tribe, so he killed the man and threw his body into a pond. Later that night other warriors from the enemy tribe came and surprised the Utes while they were sleeping. The Utes talked to them in sign language and asked them not to use their bows and arrows. The enemies said, 'We will not shoot you if you will play a hand game with us, and if you lose you must cut off your hair and give it to us.' They played the game according to the enemies' rules, and the Utes lost. Soon the enemy left, taking much long black hair with them. The Utes lost much pride that night."

THE SPIRIT THAT SINGS
MUST DANCE

The Utes shared their great love for singing and dancing with all Indians. These deeply spiritual forms of human expression held especially important significance. The outpouring of human passions such as joy, hope, anger, and fear to be found in singing and dancing served the Indian better perhaps than the written word has served western man in his attempt to explain the meaning of life. Dancing and singing or chanting is a more direct and simple expression of feeling than speech making, pictographic writing or even story telling. Dancing and singing could be vividly experienced by an entire tribe whether a Dark Ages group of cave dwellers or a sophisticated tribe of Plains Indians. Even today, it is not unusual for a younger member of the Ute tribe to suddenly and for no apparent reason break into a dance simply because he gets "the feeling."

In the old days, dances were held to celebrate all important occasions, even the tribe's arrival at a new campsite. Logically, there was also a dance performed when vacating the old campsite. Very important dances were held before leaving on the hunt to insure the killing of many animals for food. Special dances were held to build courage before battle, others were held after the battle to either celebrate a victory or to bemoan defeat. During the winter when it was difficult to hunt or gather food because of deep mountain snows, dances were held by neighboring Ute bands to facilitate courting among the young people, and to help drive away the ever present danger of famine. Sometimes dances were held in the wintertime simply to keep warm.

Some Ute dances were originally adapted from the repertoire of other tribes; a number of them found their origin among the various Plains people. Others were strictly and originally of Ute origin.

"Mamaqui Mowats," the Bear Dance, remains the most popular and well known of all Ute dances, and is still, to this day, one of the major social events of the year. It is the oldest of the known Ute dances and is performed in May or June on all three Ute reservations. Originally a very spiritual dance, the Bear Dance is now principally a social gathering where families get together with friends from their own and from other Ute reservations. Many mixed-breed Utes from outside the reservations also attend to renew old tribal ties along with guests from other tribes. The popular gathering lasts three to four days, and includes picnicking, general socializing, and a little informal trading. Origins of the Bear Dance can be traced far back into the tribal past, and although other tribes celebrate a Bear Dance, the Ute version is unique to them.

It is said that during a springtime many centuries ago, a Ute brave had a dream in which he came upon a great bear who had not yet awakened from his winter hibernation. The Ute knew that it was late in the season for the bear to be sleeping, and if not soon awakened he might starve. So, the Indian woke him from his long winter nap. As a reward for this kindness, the bear took him to a clearing deep in the woods where all the bears were dancing to celebrate the end of winter. The bears taught their Ute friend their special dance, and he then returned to his people and taught them the dance. Now, each spring, the Utes celebrate the awakening of the bears and their lasting mutual friendship by dancing.

The Bear Dance is traditionally performed inside a circular enclosure walled with six-foot cedar boughs. The single opening into the enclosure always faces the spring morning sun to the east. The dance is performed by men and women together, and the women must always invite the men to dance. Refusing to accept a dance invitation is considered an insult and is not tolerated. A dance leader, usually a medicine man or tribal elder, is armed with a willow whip and disciplines any reluctant males who are too slow in accepting a dance request. The dancing is conducted with strict decorum. The participants line up in parallel rows, with women facing men. The women wear a shawl or blanket over their shoulders in a tradition reminiscent of Spanish custom. The step is simple yet hypnotizing; three steps forward and three steps back to a slowly beating drum or morache. The most important people in-

The spring Bear Dance: the dance leader's whip helps maintain discipline.

volved in the Bear Dance are the five or six musicians or singers, because their special music must wake the bears. The bear chant has been handed down through the generations to especially designated singers, who are usually appointed to the task for life. The rasping rhythm of the accompanying morache or bear growler is created by a hard stick being drawn across the roughly notched surface of a wooden scraper or sometimes an animal's jaw bone. The drum chief is in charge of drumming for all dances, and it is his task to keep the tribal drumming equipment in good repair. At the end of the dance sessions, the musicians formally thank the tribal elders for being allowed to sing and play the sacred music. A fiesta or picnic follows the dancing, and there is socializing among old friends and courting among the young people. Although the Bear Dance is the most popular of the Ute dances, others not seen for many years are now occasionally revived in an effort to preserve the old traditions.

The Lame Dance has interesting origins. It was originally undertaken by women only. Ute women often followed the men into battle and on long hunts. After the battle or hunt, the squaws, had the weary task of carrying home whatever had been won in battle or the fresh supply of meat that had been obtained. They traveled on foot, sometimes arriving home with sore feet or lame. The Lame Dance celebrates these facts of life and perhaps represents one of the earliest women's protest demonstrations.

Various war dances were popular among the Utes, the most unique being the Scalp Dance. Surprisingly, it was also performed by women only. The dancers moved in two opposite flowing circles. The Scalp Dance celebrated a war victory and the acquisition of spoils of war, which, like most personal belongings, became the responsibility and largely the property of the women. However, if especially significant trophies had been captured during the battle, they were sometimes ceremoniously presented to the tribal elders at the climax of the dance.

Another popular form of hunting and war dance came to be known as the Dog Dance, and was performed exclusively by men. Each participant donned his full war regalia in preparation for the dance and the battle which was expected to follow. Body decorations were highly personalized, but usually included streaks of yellow and black paint, the traditional Ute war colors. The Dog Dance was adopted from Plains tribes and was danced to excite the young warriors into a state of frenzy sufficient to alleviate fear in preparation for combat.

Ute dancers in full ceremonial regalia. By 1900, Ute costumes were difficult to distinguish from those of the Plains tribes.

The Tea Dance, so-called, became very popular during the nineteenth century and was an adaptation of the strange rites the Indians observed while watching the white man's dances at trading posts and mining camps. It was danced by men and women together. Three songs were chanted, the first was accompanied by the dancers. During the second song, pipes were smoked. After the third song was chanted and danced, an herbal tea or other refreshment was served to the dancers, very reminiscent of the white man's cotillions.

The Deer Dance was first observed and reported by itinerant trappers and traders who visited the Ute camps in the Colorado mountains in the early nineteenth century. It seems to have died out with the coming of the white man. But, from early reports, it resembled "ring around the rosie" and was performed for little apparent reason whenever the Indian spirit felt the need.

Most dances held deeply spiritual meaning for the Utes and many were held in order to call upon the spirits for assistance with some problem or tribal disaster. The Round Dance was a serious ritual dance undertaken to combat illness or to alleviate a period of famine that occasionally visited the tribe. The Round Dance was led solemnly by a medicine man or healer, who was usually paid for his services. When the dance was held to cure a sick patient, the stricken man's family and friends were urged to take part. When the dance was to combat impending famine, the entire tribe became involved. Versions of the Round Dance are also popular with other tribes and can still be witnessed.

Probably the most well known of all dances performed by the western American Indian tribes is the Sun Dance. Although not vastly different from other Indian dances when normally performed, there were occasional erotic and sometimes dangerous variations incorporated into the dance by a few tribes, and for this reason, the dance acquired a somewhat sensational reputation. The Sun Dance was borrowed by the Utes from the Plains Indians and is still popular among not only the Utes, but even more so among the Sioux, Shoshone, Kiowas and many others. The Sun Dance is traditionally held at the time of the full moon and is danced by men in a virtual marathon of dance over a period of three to four days. It has very little relationship with sun worship, although the very ancient origins of the dance probably did relate to the sun's mysterious powers. The Sun Dance has always been an important dance and includes secret rites that still vary from tribe to tribe. The ritual is usually conducted around a pole or "killed" tree. The dancers fast, for the duration of the long ceremonies, taking neither food nor water, and conclude the ceremonies in near exhaustion. The form of Sun Dance held by the Utes was considered traditional or typical, and included ritual pipe smoking and many prayers to induce the appearance of great buffalo herds and an abundance of game to feed the people. The Ute version did not include erotic practices of self-torture and other violence found among a few tribes and recorded in paintings by George Catlin and others. Some bands of Sioux and Mandan and others did practice self-torture and acts of staged bravery. During these rituals bone slivers or sticks were sometimes run through the skin and attached by thongs to a pole in the center of the dance area. The participant was then suspended above the ground in excruciating pain.

George Catlin was one of the first artists to visit the western Indian tribes and to record their lives carefully on his sketch pad and canvas. On his first western trip during 1831-32 he covered 2,000 miles and traveled up the Missouri River by means of the American Fur Company's new steamboat, Yellowstone. On the return trip he traveled by canoe with two French trappers. The voyage took him through hostile Indian territory, yet Catlin stopped at many villages along the way to make detailed sketches and observations of life among the western tribes. His diaries are among the best of the period.

While visiting a large Mandan village in North Dakota, Catlin wrote this description of the Sun Dance: "I entered the medicine house . . ., and expected to see something extraordinary and strange, yet in the form of worship and devotion, but alas, little did I expect to see the interior of this temple turned into a slaughter house and its floor strewn with the blood of the fanatic devotees . . . their propitiatory suffering and tortures surpassing, if possible, the cruelty of the rack of the Inquisition . . . a number of the young men are seen reclining or fasting . . . others have been operated on by the torturers . . . one is seen sinking while the knife and splints are passed through his flesh. One is seen hanging by the splints run through the flesh of his shoulders and drawn up by men to the top of the lodge. Another is seen hung up by the pectoral muscles with four buffalo skulls attached to splints through the flesh of his arms and legs . . . another has been let down and has got strength enough to crawl to the front part of the lodge, where he is offering to the Great Spirit, the little finger of his left hand by laying it on a buffalo skull where another chops it off with a hatchet . . . while all the chiefs and dignitaries look on." The Ute people were far too practical to tolerate this sort of ritual.

The last tragic period of traditional and free tribal life came to a close towards the end of the nineteenth century, the period of the Ghost Dance. This much reported ritual dance became immensely popular throughout the west and most eloquently describes the final attempts by the Indians to save their ancient beliefs and traditional spiritualism. The Ghost Dance became uniquely intertribal and was danced by members of many western tribes, sometimes together in mixed groups. During the zenith of its popularity, small bands or single tribesmen would travel many hundreds of miles to join in and learn the dance. Even members of rival or enemy tribes were known to join together to experience the powerful dance medicine.

The Ghost Dance ritual was first created by the great Piute mystics, Wovoka and his father Tavibo. It was first performed publicly in the Walker Lake region of Nevada in 1888. It survived only through the last years of the century, but during its brief period of popularity was performed throughout the Southwest. After being outlawed by the federal government, it continued to be danced in secret ceremonies where the participants wore a magical Ghost shirt, which was thought to be impervious to bullets. The dance was created in an attempt to bring about through spiritualism and faith, a reunion with the dead, a rejuvenation of Indian society, and a restoration of the old ways, without the white men. In its failure to lift the Indian from the grip of western civilization, the Ghost Dance literally became a final symbol of the end of traditional Indian society. (See Religion and Spiritualism.)

FLUTES AND ZITHERS

The Utes found plenty of time for leisure and enjoyed music. Only a few examples of their skill at making musical instruments have been preserved. But music was often heard around campfires and was an important part of the ritual of courting and ritual services to cure the sick.

Rattles were made in various shapes and sizes, sometimes of hollowed wood or dried skins. One popular type was formed by joining two tortoise shells together with hide and thongs attached to a stick. The rattles inside were either pebbles or seeds.

A one-note wooden whistle was a popular Ute musical instrument and was sometimes used to frighten the enemy before a battle and was used to stampede buffalo herds toward an ambush.

Wooden flutes were also common and could sometimes be obtained from other tribes through itinerant traveling traders. The familiar pipestone flutes found among various tribes were occasionally obtained by trade. Local Ute models were usually made from the stem of the Yucca plant.

An unusual bowed zither was used by the Apaches and was sometimes traded to their friends the Utes. These more complex musical instruments were quite rare and very difficult to make but a few remaining examples can be found in museums. They are typically about 18" long, hollow with a slitlike sounding hole. There is an adjustable peg at one end of the sounding board which tunes a single string. The instrument is played with a crude bow. It is not known whether this unusual stringed instrument was copied from the white man's violin or was in fact developed independently.

The drum chief was an important member of every Indian group. It was his job to lead the dancing and to keep the tribal drumming equipment working and well tuned. Drums were made from various materials including hollowed logs or hides dried and stretched over a wooden frame. In addition to the most familiar types of drums the Utes borrowed a unique style from their Apache neighbors, a distinctive sounding pottery drum partially filled with water allowing the pitch to be adjusted by altering the water level.

Rare studio photo of a Ute dancer playing a flute of relatively sophisticated design. Various types were used for dancing, courting, and in battle to frighten the enemy.

HORSERACING AND
HAND GAMES

The Utes like most Indians love sports competition, and before acquiring horses from the Spanish the favorite and most popular sport was undoubtedly foot racing. Racers were trained extensively to be tough enough to run long distances and the fastest runner was an important member of his tribe. Races were run over many miles and large bets could be placed on the outcome. The fastest runner in a family or band was frequently tested against runners from other Ute groups and against challengers from other tribes. But the excitement of a tribal foot race was far surpassed in later times by an unlimited Indian passion for horse racing. Among the Utes, no sport ever approached the heights of popularity and enthusiasm lavished on the running of fast horses. In fact quarter horse racing continues to be an obsession with many Indians today.

A man with an exceptionally fast racehorse would sometimes bet all of his own and his wife's possessions on the outcome of a single important race. Occasionally, during the excitement of the race, he might even throw in his wife as part of the bet, especially if he kept more than one woman in his teepee. Ute men attached very little importance to personal posessions other than their horses. But a man's wealth and even his relative importance in the tribe could partially be measured by the number of horses he owned. Johnson, the angry medicine man who participated in the troubles at the White River Agency, owned more than 100 horses. Horses were kept in great ramudas and required much of a man's time to care for them. An 1874 estimate by the U.S. Bureau of Indian Affairs placed the total tribal horse population at over 6,000, exceeding by far the number of Ute people.

Horses were raced bareback with the rider using only a braided leather rope for control. The skillful horsemen kicked and yelled their way at full speed down a straight race course usually 200 to 300 yards long. Ute horses were known to be extremely fast, particularly in a short race. The racing characteristics of the traditional mixed-breed Indian pony have been refined and perfected into the fast-sprinting quarter horse of today.

At Ignacio, on the Southern Ute Reservation, there is a beautiful race track complete with bleachers, and adjoining it is a modern rodeo ring. Horse racing now shares popularity with rodeo.

Betting on a favorite horse was only one of many forms of gambling enjoyed by the Indians. It was common for Utes to spend many hours playing games of chance with dice or gambling sticks. The games were held in a small circle of men who were usually seated on the ground crosslegged, and the activities were sometimes accompanied by singing and drumming. Dice games usually required two dice, one black and one white, which were held by the player in his closed fist. The dice were juggled back and forth by rotating and changing the position of the hands. The watching bettors would then try to guess which hand held the dice. If the guess was wrong, the loser forfeited a gambling stick until all his sticks were gone. Gambling sticks were then exchangeable for some item among the losers' personal possessions. The early trappers claimed that Utes would bet on "anything and everything." It certainly is accurate to say that betting was part of the appeal of Ute sports.

In later years when the Utes began to socialize with trappers and white traders, they quickly learned to play card games and sometimes became addicted to faro and poker. But the Indians also devised their own card games.

Tests of physical skill accounted for a large portion of Ute sporting activity including wrestling matches and gymnastic contests. Frequently, shooting contests were held to test skills with the bow and arrow or with a lance or a gun, although rifle shooting was limited by the difficulty and great expense of obtaining ammunition. One popular event involved the challenging feat of throwing a lance through a rolling hoop. The Indians were also adept at throwing hatchets and knives at a target, and this skill was good training for battle.

Sporting events were sometimes participated in by several friendly tribes, and news of an impending get together was carried to widely separated groups by courier. The Utes held fairly regular horseracing meets near Middle Park, and these events drew Indians from hundreds of miles distance. The races could last several days or weeks with large numbers of spectators in attendance. Other events were usually held during the horserace meets and might include juggling contests in which three balls or stones were used. Bets were placed on the best performance. Climbing a greased pole was a popular contest and was frequently included in the roster of activities.

Like many tribes the Utes played an ancient form of La Crosse. It was a rough and tumble game during which bones and heads could be broken. Although usually played in a field near the campsite, it was also played on an ice-covered river or lake in winter. Perhaps not so surprisingly, the tough game of La Crosse was played mostly by women, as it is in many areas today.

Colorow, northern Ute, a familiar figure in the frontier towns and usually overweight.

MEDICINE MEN,
HOT SPRINGS, AND DEATH

Before the disruptive arrival of Europeans on the North American continent, the Indians lived in exceptionally close harmony with their environment. By natural adaptation, their bodies possessed strong immunity to disease. Although exposed to violent extremes of weather throughout their lives in a rugged mountain environment and often inadequately clothed by our standards, the Utes were surpisingly healthy people. They were admired by their Indian neighbors during the eighteenth and nineteenth centuries as a strong, vigorous tribe. When an adequate supply of meat and wild plant foods was available, the Ute thrived in his chosen life style. Only when extreme drought descended upon the region did the Utes and their neighbors become weakened and experience increased sickness.

Most common diseases imported by the European immigrants were completely unknown to the Indians. Therefore, they possessed almost no natural immunity to such European-introduced diseases as measles, mumps, and smallpox, etc. When a steamboat rumbled up the Missouri River in 1837 belching smoke and carrying a load of trappers and traders, it also carried an epidemic of smallpox on board. The resulting infection of the Mandan tribe that lived in villages along the river in South Dakota reduced the tribal population of 1,600 to 1,800 to a reported 120 survivors and almost destroyed their ancient and unusually sophisticated culture.

Sickness and its cures were closely related to Indian spiritualism and to religion. When a member of the tribe became ill, his body was considered to be out of tune with nature. It had been entered by bad spirits either self caused or the evil spirits could have been induced into his body by an enemy. Usually the services of a medicine man or shaman were called for when the illness was serious. The medicine man first made careful preparation of a variety of paraphernalia which he carried with him in a special leather pouch.

The Utes believed that medical treatment was more successful if given at night. The Navajos, on the other hand, began their medical treatment with a curative sand painting created in front of the sick patient's residence, and this had to be completed before dark in order to be effective. Sand painting is still an important part of Navajo medicine, and the intricate and complex ritual designs are carefully handed down to apprentice practitioners by each successive generation. There is little evidence that the Utes used sand painting as a part of their medicine except in very isolated cases. The Ute medicine man quite often used dreams as part of his special cure. Sometimes he would observe absolute silence during his treatment speaking only through an assistant. A typical treatment might include the shaman's forcing himself into a trancelike state during prolonged praying and singing. The patient's relatives and friends were often called upon to assist with the cure by joining the chanting or dancing. Assistance from as many relatives as possible also helped to spread the blame around, in case the treatments ended in failure or in the death of the patient. There were many specific rituals and special medicines for different types of maladies. A full treatment might last all night or could continue for several days and nights, depending upon the severity of the illness. Sometimes herbal medicines were used; at other times ritual pipe smoking might be prescribed to supplement curative herb potions.

One peculiar type of treatment reached its climax when the medicine man simply pressed the top of his own head against the sick spot on the patient's body, thus transferring his own body force to the afflicted area. The medicine man then ceremoniously spit from his mouth the source of the sickness. According to an early eyewitness report, another treatment included stomping on the patient and then grasping him by the shoulders and rocking his body back and forth to knock out the evil spirits.

A prescription of herbs or poultices was often left for the patient, to be administered by the family according to careful instructions. A prescription could include painting the patient's face red in some specific pattern or more effectively, the prescription might call for the avoidance of certain foods. Intense and lengthy ritual prayers by the squaws and other members of the family were required in some cases. If the situation really got desperate, the shaman might even change the patient's name. Indian medical practitioners were surprisingly successful and might be richly paid for their services. They often acquired great wealth in horses and other gifts as their reputation grew. But, occasionally, the role of a medicine man could become an extremely dangerous profession. If he continued to lose too many patients and was therefore adjudged by the tribal elders to be an evil shaman, he could be summarily killed by members of the offended patient's family.

Spiritualism and faith in one's self certainly plays a role in curing sickness, and the many successes of faith healing have never been fully understood. A mental process not unlike the stoicism and positive thinking practiced by Christian Scientists today seems to have played an important part in Indian medicine. Modern medical science is finally, now, beginning to understand the importance of mental attitude as a cause and cure of illness.

There were many practical and effective Indian remedies, some of which were adopted by the early white settlers; and a few are still in use by modern medicine. Spearmint was regularly gathered to soothe an upset stomach and was widely traded between the tribes. Grease and flour were plastered over a wound to effectively stop bleeding. Skunk grease was used to soften and soothe chapped hands in winter time. Potato dipped in a vinegar solution could be an effective headache remedy. Sagebrush could be chewed or brewed into a tea for use in fighting winter colds. Flour or corn meal browned with grease and water was taken to curb diarrhea. Tobacco packed into an aching tooth was used to pull out the pain. Many of these remedies are effective and are still used by the Indians and in some rural white areas.

There were many superstitions related to the mysteries of sickness and physical disabilities. A father who placed his hands to his ears while his wife was pregnant might cause deafness in the child. If dogs howled or coyotes came closer to camp than usual and howled, it could mean that death was near. A squaw who was foolish enough to sweep the floor at night might be severely beaten by her husband because this could loose evil spirits upon the family. Evil spirits were much more active at night, reflecting the universal human fear of darkness, and many folk tales refer to their nocturnal activities.

Although generally a very healthy group of people, the Utes did have certain health problems. Common among them was toothache and other tooth-related infections due in part to the rough foods that were a regular part of their diet. They were also frequent victims of rheumatism and arthritis, sometimes at quite young ages, and seem to have been occasionally infected with oesteomylitis, a crippling disease of the bone marrow. The Utes also suffered from birth defects and frequent stomach disorders.

A very popular cure for general body pain was the sweat house. It was usually a small enclosed pit or wickiup covered over with tree branches and plastered over the top with thick mud. A fire was built in the center of the hut around which two or more people would sit. Hot stones thrust into water supplied clouds of steam. The sweat house enjoyed the same popularity as saunas today, but were more commonly used by the Indians to cure sickness.

The Utes were lucky to own within their vast mountain empire numerous natural hot springs. These were used extensively by the tribe and were guarded jealously against unfriendly intruders. Rheumatism and arthritis were frequent cripplers, and trips to a hot spring were considered important to general health. Chief Ouray of the Tabeguach Utes suffered from chronic rheumatism during much of his adult life and during his last years was carried on a horse-drawn travois from his home near Montrose, Colorado, to the active hot springs, at present Hot Sulphur Springs, for treatment.

The hot springs were such an important segment of Ute activity that during the 1700s and early 1800s some were extensively fortified by the construction of long, reinforced stone ballistrades to keep out enemy tribes. Small fortifications built for this purpose have been found near Granby and on Williams Fork and near Manitou Springs west of present Colorado Springs. The soothing, healing hot springs were often the scene of skirmishes between the Utes and their rival neighbors. Only hunting territory and horses were more jealously coveted than the hot springs.

Samuel Bowles, in his book, *Our New West*, written in 1869, recalls coming upon a large group of Ute teepees housing about 600 people, encamped near Hot Sulphur Springs, Colorado. They had been hunting in Middle Park and enjoying the warm spring waters. He recalls that the women traded raspberries for biscuits and honey, and were scrupulously honest. At the spring there were Indians apparently suffering from dyspepsia and undoubtedly arthritis and some had bad coughs. He notes that the Indians even treated their sick horses in the springs. He also notes that the Utes generally had fine features and particularly clear, piercing eyes. Bowles summarizes his impressions with this: "The incongruous mixture of white men's food and clothing and lifestyle, with their own, which their contact with civilization has led them to, is sapping their vitality at its foundations."

Colorow, a leader of the Yampa band of Utes, recalled from his childhood a battle between his clan of northern Utes and a very bold hunting party of Arapahoes who had traveled the long distance from the plains of eastern Colorado through Ute territory to hunt in the Roaring Fork Valley and use the well-known Yampa Springs at present Glenwood Springs. Colorow's band was surprised by the sudden appearance of the Arapahoes and were forced to barricade themselves on Red Mountain near Carbondale. When reinforcements finally arrived, the Utes were able to drive off the intruders.

There were many stories about the colorful Colorow who was a garrulous and popular leader and reportedly had been captured from the Comanches as a baby. He became a familiar character among white settlers all the way from Denver to Glenwood Springs.

One day, when Colorow was quite elderly and had grown in girth and weighed 250 pounds, he visited the new town of Glenwood Springs in order to again use the hot springs that had by then become a tourist attraction. He supposedly told this story to a visitor at the elaborate new Hotel Colorado. Years before, he said, a white girl had wandered away from her family while they were traveling west through Ute territory on their way to California. She was found wandering alone on the trail by a then young Colorow and his family, and was adopted by them. Colorow soon fell in love with the young girl and married her. Her name was Recha. Colorow gave her a horse and they traveled together for many years. One day near the Yampa Springs, Recha was thrown from her horse and killed. Colorow was grief stricken and buried his white wife above the springs. He never again returned to the Yampa Springs until he grew old and then only returned to tell the story. Colorow was also known for telling tall tales to the tourists.

The Utes extensively used the hot springs on the San Juan River and the many springs found on the tributaries of the Grand River (Colorado River). Perhaps the most popular of all the springs was the Fontaine qui Bouille (the fountain that boils) near Colorado Springs. Called Manitou Springs by the Indians, after the great God, Manitou, this famous spa was considered sacred and was claimed equally by the Utes and Arapahoes.

Manitou Springs was the scene of many skirmishes between the two hated rivals and between other Plains tribes that occasionally visited the popular spot. A small fortification was built by the Indians near the springs for protection while using the waters. It was a circular stone barricade large enough to hold three or four men. At different times it was apparently used by many tribes, none of which were known for the building of stone works.

The life expectancy of the Indians was short by our standards, and many Indians appeared aged beyond their years, particularly women, although this was not always the case. Diseases of aging were common, and arthritis and rheumatism were particularly widespread.

Captain Gunnison's journal describes a chance meeting between his survey party and a group of aged Ute women near the Grand River (Colorado). The young women apparently fled into the brush with their children upon the approach of his party but the old women were too feeble and slow and stayed behind. "They were small in stature and bent forward with the years, wearing their coarse hair, still abundant, cut short across the forehead. . . . Their features are dried and shrunken to a mummy-like appearance with bleared eyes and sunken lips covering teeth worn to the gums [from eating abrasive foods]. The joints of their fingers are stiff and distorted and all are enlarged."

Death was a great mystery to the Utes and was deeply feared by most Indians. Therefore, burials were an unpleasant task and were usually accomplished in great haste. The dead were sometimes placed in shallow earth graves or were buried in a natural cave or a crevice in the rocks, which was then sealed with stones. Cremation was also practiced. The body might be placed in a cedar tree with brush piled against it; the tree was then burned. Burial platforms were occasionally used to elevate the body away from marauding animals and to place the spirit closer to the Happy Hunting Ground in the sun. Sometimes the dead tribesman's horse and dog were killed and included in the burial in order to serve their master in the next world. Personal belongings such as pipes, atlatls, or bows and arrows and pots and other cooking utensils were broken, or "killed," and also placed with the burial for use in the next life. Burial locations were considered to possess especially dangerous magic and were rarely visited by the living. Contamination of a burial site was considered a despicable sacrilege and if caused by an enemy was adequate provocation for going to war.

GRASSHOPPERS AND CAMERASS ROOT

Good diet certainly creates a stronger society, and this historical platitude is verified by the progress of the Ute people. Before the arrival of the Europeans with their domesticated horses, the Utes survived on a relatively limited diet restricted to the animals that could be easily hunted on foot, and the wild plants gathered over a relatively small land area. The tribe was traditionally a group of gatherers and hunters rather than farmers.

Normally the gathering of food consumed most of the tribe's productive time. Wild roots, berries, and various grasses were obtained fairly easily, but only during the short mountain summer season. The growing season in the best hunting areas of the Colorado Rockies is only of 10 to 12 weeks' duration due to the cold and high altitude. Fish and small game could be hunted and trapped most of the year, except in times of extreme drought, and the deer and elk were carefully followed on their annual migrations on foot.

About 1640, the Utes began to acquire horses from the Spanish and became one of the first North American Indian tribes to be mounted on these wonderful "magic dogs." Their mobility allowed them to follow the large herds of migrating elk and deer and buffalo more easily as they roamed the high plateau country in search of the best grasses. With larger supplies of red meat added to their daily food supply, the tribe began to gain stature and to enjoy increasingly better health. Within a relatively short period after becoming horse owners, the Utes were reported in the Spanish chronicles as a relatively strong, taller, and better-looking people than earlier Spanish reports had described them. Larger quantities of wild fruits and berries could now be gathered in the summer over a wider area by mounted tribesmen. With extended travel, trade increased and occasionally even peaches could be bought or stolen from Navajo fruit orchards in far-off Canyon de Chelly. Although Utes raised very little produce themselves, except for a rare patch of corn or squash, they were able to trade for field crops such as beans and corn and squash from the more sedentary neighboring southern tribes in northern New Mexico and Arizona.

Food was gathered in season and then stored for future use in secret caches along regularly used trails so that supplies would be available during later seasonal migrations. A variety of wild roots were staples of the Indian diet. The Utes made a dried cake from the root of the Yampa plant, a member of the carrot family, and sometimes this was mixed with tobacco root and camerass root for flavor. Camas bulbs, a member of the lily family, grew wild near water and were considered a delicacy. The women gathered many different seeds from wild grasses in their woven burden baskets, and these were pounded into meal. Pinon nuts were a popular delicacy, and even the pitch from the pinon pine tree was useful as a waterproofing for water jug baskets. The black dye obtained from the versatile pinon was used for textiles and for war paint. Strips of the tender bark of pine trees could be flavored with salt and eaten. Sap from the aspen tree, a cousin of the poplars and cottonwoods, was collected and included in the Indian diet. The mahogany-colored fruit of the prickly pear cactus was carefully harvested when ripe, but had to be boiled before eating. The yucca plant, which grows both in the form of small bushes and also can become thick trees, is a strange non-conforming member of the lily family. It produced a great variety of supplies, including food, needles for sewing, fiber for making sandals and baskets, and a root which could be turned into a fine soap. Sandals made of yucca fiber are still occasionally discovered in archealogical digs after surviving for hundreds of years. The tanagre root, which is rich in tannin, was used widely by the western tribes as a tooth cleanser.

Meat, of course, was the mainstay of the Utes' protein-rich diet and was consumed in large quantities. It was either roasted on a spit over a fire or boiled. After boiling, the meat was pounded until it became soft, much like modern tenderizing, and then rolled in meat greases. The rolled meat product with its thick coating of fat could be stored for long periods for use in the winter when game could not be easily hunted. Fat was also used for cleansing the body and for insulation against the cold. Trimmed off boiled meat, the fat was smeared on the body and then scraped off with a bone or shell scrapper providing a good non-frigid bath, and at the same time by clinging to the pores of the skin, it provided extra warmth in the winter.

Apparently, only the Uintah Utes ate grasshoppers, a habit learned from their poor Piute cousins who scratched out a bare living for centuries on the arid semi-desert of central Utah and eastern Nevada. The legs were torn off and the bodies were covered with hot ashes. When cooked, the grasshoppers were laboriously ground into a meaty substance that is very rich in protein.

Some fishing was done with the bow and arrow or with a spear, a skill which required great patience and good marksmanship. The Indians also made finely carved fish hooks and fish traps, and these were sometimes traded between tribes. But, fish were not a favorite food of the meat-loving Utes, and they fished mainly when game was scarce.

Buffalo and deerskin became the Ute's principal trade goods after arrival of the white man, and the tribe became wealthy from the exportation of these animal by-products. The great roaming buffalo herds supplied thick hides for teepees and warm winter cloaks and robes to wear and to sleep in. The horns and hooves and bone of the buffalo were turned into strong household utensils, and the muscle and sinew were used for tough bindings and for thread and bow strings. Smoked and dried buffalo meat (jerky) was carried on long journeys providing instant meals and could be easily stored for winter. Buffalo chips were used as an efficient fuel.

Food gathering became far simpler for the Utes on horseback than ever before and gave them more leisure time. The rich natural resources of the Colorado mountains provided them with a reliable diet, although famine conditions did occasionally threaten after a particularly hard winter or drought-stricken summer. But even in times of famine, the horse gave the mobility necessary to save lives, thus the Utes enjoyed a more reliable food supply than many of their neighbors. Adequate food contributed to the mountain-dwelling Utes' generally easy going nature and undoubtedly accounts for their ability to survive longer than other tribes without assistance from the white man, as the tide of migrating settlers and prospectors slowly, but systematically, destroyed the natural food supplies of the nearby plains and deserts.

Ute beaded moccasins. The flower designs were borrowed from the Iroquois and the French Canadian missionaries. Note the ceremonial pair with fully beaded soles.

BUCKSKIN AND
WATER JUG BASKETS

Every utensil and every item of clothing and weapon used by the Indian household had to be made by hand or obtained from other tribal groups by trading. In perfecting their skills as traders, the Utes learned that leather was a most sought-after product, particularly by the Spanish. Prepared deerskin became the Utes' cash crop, and the Ute leather trade is referred to many times in Spanish colonial records. Deer and elk were abundant in the Rocky Mountains and provided an easily obtained supply of fine skins. The Utes became renowned for their outstanding leather-tanning skills.

In the old days when the Utes were less mobile, the preparation of deerskin was usually carried out by the men of the tribe. Later, however, when horses became the great symbol of wealth, the task of tanning skins was to a large extent turned over to the women. The preparation was a tedious and fairly complex process. Fresh deerhide was first carefully cleaned with a large bone scraper to eliminate the flesh and hair. It was then soaked overnight in water and subsequently wrung dry by twisting tightly with the aid of a stick. Next, deer brains were rubbed thoroughly into the skin using a bunch of juniper as a rubbing tool. The hide was then staked out in the sun to dry for several days. A second time, the hide was soaked in water and again set out in the sun. While still damp, the curing skin was fully stretched by placing one end between the feet and pulling over and over again. The tiresome stretching process took about half a day to complete. The hide was then smoked.

This was the critical part of the tanning process and had to be done carefully. The hide was propped over a small fire heating and cooking for about one-half hour until the proper color was obtained in the skin. Different wood smoke created different shades of coloring in the final leather product. Willow smoke turned the hide brown, pine smoke was used to turn it a light yellow and greasewood turned it a darker yellow. A final part of the tanning process involved rubbing fine white clay into the skin with a flat stone. This sealed the pores and improved the smooth texture of the finished leather.

The leather-making skills of the Ute tribe also extended to the making of good quality doeskin and buckskin clothing, but mainly for their own consumption. Moccasins and buckskin shirts and leggings, gauntlets, quivers, pipe bags and many other items of the finest quality were made from Ute deer skins. Finished deerskin was eagerly sought by Spanish and American craftsmen and was made into expensive buckskin and doeskin clothing for people of the growing frontier towns. These products were sometimes shipped east to distant markets and even to Europe.

Intricate and beautifully executed beadwork was also associated with the Utes, and for a time the tribe made significant amounts of beaded clothing. This craft was passed to them by the Plains tribes, who in turn learned beadwork from the Indians of the northeastern United States, and in particular the Iroquois nation. Beautifully beaded moccasins, shirts, quiver cases, and cradleboard decorations made by the Utes are among the very best to be found anywhere. There is little evidence that beadwork was created by the tribe before 1860, and by 1930 Ute beadwork was pretty much a lost art. But in the intervening years, the Utes quickly realized the high value of beaded buckskin and beaded cloth and established a brisk trade with tribes to the south. Ute beadwork was also sought by white traders who paid good prices. The squaws began to produce large quantities of colorful beaded belts, pouches, charms, and finely designed hat bands strictly for trading purposes. Beautiful ceremonial moccasins were sometimes beaded over the entire surface of the sole and heel in intricate designs. Some, but not enough, fine Ute beadwork has been preserved in museums. Some of the best examples of beaded Ute shirts, leggings, and dresses can be seen in the excellent collection housed at the Denver Art Museum.

Indian beadwork first began to be produced contemporarily with the earliest Indian contacts with explorers who brought the craft with

Ute fringed, doeskin dress with the entire top beautifully beaded. The cross is a life symbol of the four winds.

them from Europe. The first traders who landed on the New England and Virginia shores brought colorful Venetian glass beads, which were offered as gifts to the tribes they encountered. Glass beadwork had been popular in Europe for centuries as an adornment for women's clothing. The Iroquois Indians later became known for their handsome beadwork purses and ornamented articles of clothing prepared for the tourist trade and often distinguished by beautiful floral designs taught to them by the missionary nuns of the French Canadian convents. The skill slowly moved west with the traders and with the forced westward migrations of the east coast tribes.

By 1930, beadwork was no longer fashionable in the cities of America and the demand for it almost ceased to exist. There remained very little incentive for Indian women to make beaded products because by that time even traditional Indian clothing was worn only on ceremonial occasions. In recent years however, the Ute tribal council has made some effort to revive the craft, but with only limited success.

The Utes made very little pottery, largely because of their life style. Pottery was easily broken, and therefore impractical for a tribe constantly on the move. Basket making, on the other hand, was an ancient and well-developed skill practiced throughout Ute history and into the early twentieth century. Lightweight woven reed containers and baskets were far more practical for a nomadic tribe following the wild game herds.

Basketry made by the Utes and baskets made by their close friends, the Apaches, can be very similar in both quality and design and attests to the long standing relationship between the two neighboring Indian groups. The Utes produced large finely woven burden baskets and berry picking baskets sometimes three to four feet tall. They were made to be carried on the back, attached with a leather harness. Large storage baskets and water jug baskets were also produced in quantity as mainstays of household equipment. The familiar coiled baskets were usually made of squaw brush when the finest quality was desired, while thin willow branches were used for more coarse basketry. Squaw brush was best gathered in the spring when it was soft and supple and was stored until needed. Before weaving, the material was soaked in water to make it more pliable. Sometimes colored designs were woven into the baskets by inserting vegetable-dyed colored strands, and these fine patterns have made the few remaining examples of old Ute basketry very valuable.

Later, in order to satisfy the increasing demand for trade goods, designs were sometimes simply painted onto the basket surface with dyes, but this quick method resulted in an inferior product.

Water jug baskets were very important to the migrating Utes, because the lightweight vessels could be easily carried on one's back or on a dog-powered travois without fear of breaking. Water jugs were tightly woven in the normal coiled fashion with a narrowed neck at the top, and were then thoroughly lined on the inside with hot liquid pine pitch. During the application of hot pitch, the basket was rolled back and forth to insure that all crevices were thoroughly sealed. Sometimes the exterior of the jug was also covered with pitch and then rubbed with a coating of clay for additional strength. These tough woven water jugs were practically indestructible and are occasionally still found in use. Buckskin pouches were also used for carrying water and for food and other burdens, but it was more difficult to keep them watertight.

Although not a pottery-making people, the Utes did occasionally create crude pottery strictly for their own use. Pottery making was observed at some Ute encampments by the earliest beaver trappers who visited Colorado in the 1820s and 30s, but the skill was not well developed. The art of making pottery was highly developed among the Anasazi people (old people) of the Four Corners region of Arizona and New Mexico, from whom the Utes may be partially descended, and was carried on and vastly improved by the settled tribes of the pueblos. The Navajos, Hopis, and Zunis continue to perfect these skills and turn out beautifully decorated and finished pottery today.

Ironically, the Ute tribe has begun to turn out commercial pottery with Indian-type designs at a small factory on the Ute Mountain Reservation. The attractive product is becoming popular, but does not reflect traditional Ute culture.

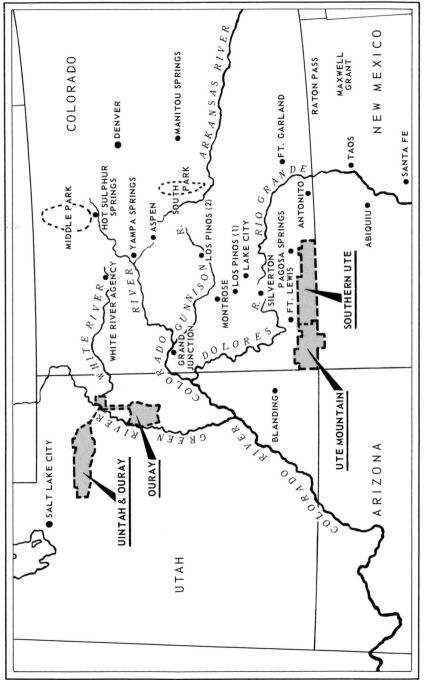

PRESENT-DAY UTE INDIAN TERRITORY

HOW THE OWL HAWKS
TRICKED TUVAT AINC

Storytelling, religious symbolism, superstition and patterns of social behavior were very closely associated elements of Ute Indian culture. Nature-oriented beliefs lend themselves to the use of storytelling as a means of transmitting ideas. The Utes handed down many ancient tales about animals and birds, the earth and sky, and stories about storms and the weather. These folktales had a single thread of common purpose that reflected a strong harmony between man and the elements of nature.

In the absence of a written language the Ute family elders became the teachers and as such they were especially revered, particularly if they happened to be especially good storytellers. Itinerant Indian traders who occasionally traveled from tribe to tribe, were expected to be good storytellers, too. Sometimes these roving peddlers roamed over great distances, visiting tribes from the Mississippi River to the California coast. Evidence of this far-flung yet sporadic trade has been proven by the discovery of shell goods and other trade items from far distant origins. The occasional contact by traders caused a cross-pollenization of stories and ideas between various tribes and brought their cultures closer together. Intermarriage between tribes, when it occurred, had a similar affect in bringing far-flung and isolated tribes like the Utes culturally close to the Plains tribes.

Social ethics, religion, hunting skills, bravery, and even mechanical skills were taught orally through stories. The subject of these folk tales with a purpose might be men but they could just as easily be told about animals, birds, and even insects. Inevitably, superstition played an important role in Indian behavior and mystic beliefs were perpetuated down the centuries through legend and the telling of ghost stories.

Frightening and blood-curdling stories were told about fierce Navajo warriors and about the treacherous Arapahoes, who were more or less perpetual enemies of the Utes. It was thought that members of these enemy tribes could cast evil spells over people who came in contact with them. There were many stories tailored especially for children and most served an educational purpose beyond entertainment, such as, lessons about safety, good health, or even hunting skills.

Pa ah a pache or "the water baby" is an evil spirit that dwells deep in rivers and lakes. It can snatch small Indian children into the water if they step too close, or can even catch them at night on dry land if they are not properly home in their beds. It is an interesting sidelight that many western Indians did not learn how to swim.

Se Ach is a cruel and wily witch with fishlike scales and red eyes that hang on cords from her head. Her specialty is cooking and eating unruly children. Tales of witches and spirits were often surprisingly similar even when told by tribes living thousands of miles apart. Many superstitions involved the making of war, romance, and simple everyday conduct, and these were handed down for countless generations. Birds flying into the house are omens of bad luck and especially bad luck is an owl's hoot. Some tribes living in Canada believe the owl is capable of repeating the name of a person who will die soon, therefore the owl is considered particularly ominous. Never look an owl straight in the eye because his stare can cast evil spells.

A Ute would never whistle or comb his hair at night. Mirrors are known to be dangerous because they attract lightning; so will dogs when allowed in the house. Dreams about blood or the color red are extremely hazardous and should immediately be retold to the entire family in order to diminish the power of the evil spirits the dream has aroused.

Favorite stories were repeated generation after generation from grandfathers to sons and daughters, and when stories were sometimes borrowed from another tribe they were always told with a special local flavor or twist. Many stories were told about the prowess of animals such as the clever coyote and the bear and about the wisest of all animals, the mountain lion. Stories of brave warriors and of battles won and lost form the slim basis of Indian history and are essential in attempting to trace tribal backgrounds. Memories of famines and floods and of especially good buffalo hunts were told and retold. Stories, folk tales and pictographs found carefully drawn on cave walls and canyon faces provide the main source from which early Indian history is being slowly pieced together. Unfortunately, such historical clues are scarce and much of the fascinating Indian past will never be known.

For years the Utes would not go near Grand Lake near present Granby, Colorado, because it was considered haunted. Once a Ute hunting party was camped on the shores of this beautiful lake. The men were scattered in the nearby forest looking for game and had left their teepees unprotected. Suddenly, without warning the peaceful encampment was attacked by a strong war band of Arapahoes. The Ute women and children hastily scrambled onto a makeshift raft lying by the shore of the lake and poled and pushed themselves far out into deep water for safety. Hearing the screams of their women, the Ute men soon returned and began to drive the Arapahoe enemies away. But a strong summer windstorm suddenly came up over the lake, and the water was soon churned into choppy waves. The crowded raft capsized, drowning most of the women and children in the frigid water. For many years afterwards, Grand Lake was considered haunted by the spirits of the dead and therefore considered unsafe to visit.

The so-called radium hot springs at Hot Sulphur Springs, Colorado, are still said to be heated by the magic fire of an ancient Ute chief because of a tragedy that occurred there. Long before the white man came, a wise old chief enjoyed visiting the warm springs to soothe his tired body. One day he was joined at the spring by a band of young warriors. The young men were restless and wanted to cross over the mountains to the east in order to raid the encampment of a neighboring tribe where they believed they could capture many horses. The old chief warned that the enemy tribe was too strong to be successfully attacked and that such a dangerous trip would result in all of them being killed. The young men would not listen, and when the old chief refused to lead them, they appointed a new war chief to take them. The old chief was very distressed but promised to wait for their return at his campfire by the spring. Of course, the foolish warriors never returned. But the old chief still waits for them and his campfire still burns at the water's edge, perpetually warming the spring.

The Puma (mountain lion) had a wife and son whom he loved very much. One day he went into the woods to hunt for rabbits with his son. While they were away from the home the black bear came to the Puma's tent. He saw the Puma's beautiful wife alone, and immediately fell in love with her. "I wish to have this woman," he thought to himself enviously. Finally, the bear pursuaded her to run away with him. Soon, the Puma returned to his home and found his wife missing and he was very angry. He could smell the bear's scent and he immediately set out in pursuit of his new enemy and trailed the bear for two long days. Finally, he came upon the bear and his wife resting in a cedar grove. The bear had been saying to her, "I am stronger than the Puma." But the Puma's wife had replied, "No, you are in danger because he is stronger than you." Then the Puma entered the cedar grove. The bear heard the Puma approaching and quickly put on his moccasins in order to run to safety, but in his haste he put them on the wrong feet. Thus, the Puma easily caught the bear. He furiously wrestled the bear to the ground and soon broke the bear's back. Then he caught his unfaithful wife and threw her to the ground and broke her back. He then went away sadly with his son and never returned to that part of the country.

Ten insects (Tuvat ainc) killed a white-tail deer one day. Two owl hawks watched them do it and decided to trick the insects into giving up their valuable catch. So, they approached and said, "Tuvat ainc, why did you kill our brother the deer? You have displeased us by this cruel act and you must go away so that we can bury him properly." The insects could not understand this strange request, and answered, "The deer cannot be your brother. You do not look anything like him. You have wide eyes and feathers and wings." "No, no," answered the owl hawks, "he is our brother but he has lived far away from us in the willows for many years. That is why he looks so different. Anyway, if you do not go away and leave him for us, we will shoot you."

So, the 10 insects went away thinking the owl hawks would build a fire and burn their brother's body for a proper burial. Instead, the owl hawks built a fire to deceive the insects, but then they carried the deer home to eat. They laughed for a long time about the insects. "We tricked them," they said, "white-tailed deer always tastes good."

EPILOGUE

Observing these quiet people, the Ute Indians, it is easy to lament or condemn their sometimes indifferent attitude toward the loss of their unique culture. It is also easy to forget how the "old ways" were stolen from them by western civilization and by a United States government whose vacillating policies continue to be debilitating rather than constructive. Government policy, which for many years was highlighted by neglect, has now taken a guilt ridden "about face," which is equally destructive to the Indians. Vast sums of federal dollars and energy payments from private industry are pouring into the tribal treasury. In some ways, the tribal leaders are still ill-equipped to make good use of this new largess. In spite of new financial security and successful business and community programs, the problems of school dropouts, alchoholism, suicide, and lack of incentive to lead productive lives continue to inhibit social progress.

Yet, looking beyond their vanishing cultural heritage and many lingering problems, it is not difficult to admire the enduring Ute people and their less complicated life-style which is still more family- and community-oriented and, comparatively speaking, less materialistic than that of their Caucasian neighbors.

BIBLIOGRAPHY

Barber, Edwin. 1876. "Language and Utensils of the Modern Utes." Bulletin of the U.S. Geological and Geographical Survey.

Bowles, Samuel. 1869. *Our New West*. Hartford: Hardford Publishing Company.

Breternitz, David. 1975. "Mesa Verde, The Green Table." National Park Service.

Brown, Dee. 1971. *Bury My Heart at Wounded Knee*. New York: Holt, Rinehart, and Winston.

Casey, Pearle. 1938. "Buckskin Charley, Chief of the Utes." *Southwestern Lore* IV.

Catlin, George. 1845. *Illustrations of the Manners and Customs of the North American Indians*. London: Bohn.

Ceram, C. W. 1971. *The First American*. New York: Harcourt, Brace, Jovanovich.

Cerquone, Joseph. *The Dominguez-Escalante Expedition*.

Chapin, Frederick. 1892. *Land of the Cliff Dwellers*. Appalachian Mountain Club Publishing Company.

Delaney, Robert. 1974. *The Southern Ute People*. Indian Tribal Series.

Freeman, Dan. 1962. *Four Years with the Utes*. Waco: Morrison Publishing Company.

Fremont, John. 1845. *Exploration and Survey*. U.S. War Department.

Gunnison, John. 1854. *Exploration and Survey*. U.S. War Department.

Hallenbeck. 1940. *Journey of Cabeza de Vaca*. Clark Publishing Company.

Howbert, Irving. 1914. *Indians of the Pike Peak Region*. Rio Grande Press.

Jackson and Spence. *Expedition of John C. Fremont*. University of Illinois Press.

Jackson, D., ed. 1966. *Journals of Zebulon Pike*. University of Oklahoma Press.

Jackson, Wm. H. 1940. *Time Exposure*. New York: G.P. Putnam's Sons.

Jackson, Wm. H. 1938. "A Visit to the Los Pinos Indian Agency." *Colorado Magazine*.

Jefferson and Delaney and Thompson. 1972. *The Southern Utes: A Tribal History*. Ignacio: Southern Ute Tribe.

Jocknick, Sydney, ed. 1968. *Fireside Chats with Otto Mears*.

Long, Haniel. "Cabeza de Vaca, Interlinear of Journey from Florida." *Santa Fe*.

Look, A. 1972. *The Utes' Last Stand*. The Golden Bell Press.

Lowie, R. H. 1954. "Indians of the Plains." American Museum of Natural History.

Lyman. 1964. *The Ute People, An Historical Study and Bibliographical Checklist.* Provo: Brigham Young University.

McConnel, Virginia. 1963. *Ute Pass: Route of the Sky People.* Sage Books.

McCrackin, H. 1952. *Portrait of the Old West.* New York: McGraw-Hill.

Malouf, Carling. 1945. "The Effects of Spanish Slavery on the Indians." *Southwest Journal of Anthropology.*

Meriwether, David. 1965. *My Life in the Mountains and Plains.* University of Oklahoma Press.

Miles, Charles. 1963. *Indian Artifacts in North America.* Bonanza Publishing Company.

Oliva, Leo. 1967. *Soldiers of the Santa Fe Trail.* University of Oklahoma Press.

Rockwell. 1956. *The Utes, a Forgotten People.* Sage Books.

Safe, Rufus. 1857. *Rocky Mountain Life.* Hewes and Company.

Smith Anne. *Ethnology of the Northern Utes.* The Museum of New Mexico Press.

Southern Ute Tribe. 1960. "Where We Stand Now: A Report." Ignacio: Southern Ute Tribe.

Sprague, Marshall. 1976. *Colorado.* Norton Press.

Strong, P. 1946. *Horses and Americans.* Garden City Publishing Company.

Terrell, John. 1962. *Journey into Darkness.* New York: William Morrow.

"Uintah Indian Survey." 1903.

Ute Tribal Council. 1977. *Ute-Comanche Peace Treaty Ceremony.* Southern Ute Tribe.

Watson, Don. 1961. *Indians of Mesa Verde.* Mesa Verde Museum Association.

NEWSPAPERS

The Aspen Times

The Rocky Mountain News (early editions: 1859).

Also, Thanks to help from:

American Museum of Natural History, New York, N.Y.
Aspen Public Library, Aspen, Colorado.
Colorado State Historical Society, Denver, Colorado.
Denver Public Library, Denver, Colorado.
Heye Museum of the American Indian, New York, N.Y.
New Mexico Historical Library & Museum, Santa Fe, N.M.
New Mexico State Archives, Santa Fe, N.M.

INDEX

De Niza, Father Marcos, 14
De Onate, Juan, 15
De Rivera, Juan, 29
De Rosas, Luis, 7, 15
De Vaca, Cabeza, 12-14
De Vargas, Diego, 26, 30, 145
Deerskin, 88, 119, 133, 143, 171, 173-74
Delgadito, 19, 35
Denver, Colorado, 3, 4, 8, 12, 38, 55, 56, 57, 65, 72, 79, 80, 81, 89, 90, 92, 99, 109, 111, 113, 144, 167
Divorce, 139
Dodge, F.S., 96
Dominguez-Escalante Expedition, 31-35
Dominguez, Francisco, 4, 29, 31, 32, 33
Douglas (Quinkent), 21, 64, 72, 89, 90, 94, 95, 97, 98
Durango, Colorado, 97

El Albo, 35
Escalante, Father Silvestre, 4, 31, 32
Espanola, N.M., 42
Estivanico, 14
Evans, John, 65

Fauntleroy, Thomas, 51
Forth Duchesne, Utah, 107, 124-26, 124
Fort Garland, Colorado, 50, 51, 73, 80
Fort Lewis, Colorado, 97, 119
Fort Massachusetts, 50
Four Corners, 1, 8, 10, 11, 114, 177
Fowler, Jacob, 39
Fremont, John C., 11, 43, 47, 50

Ghost Dance, 132, 133, 135, 156
Ghost Dance Society, 133, 135
Ghosts, 131, 180
Glenwood Springs, Colorado, 67,
73, 111, 167
Graham, Benjamin, 73
Grand Junction, Colorado, 41, 55, 67, 101, 119, 120
Grand Lake, Colorado, 12, 181
Grand Mesa, 32, 97, 99, 107
Grand River (Colorado River), 32, 54, 57, 67, 97, 167, 168
Grand River band, 21, 67
Grant, U.S., 65, 66, 73
Greeley, Horace, 67, 86, 87
Guadalupe-Hidalgo, Treaty of, 42, 43
Guera Morah (Salvadore), 43, 57, 60
Guerro, 72, 77, 82
Gunnison, John, 52, 54, 168

Hayden, F.V., Expedition, 70, 73, 74
Hayes, Rutherford, 64, 65, 105
Hopi, 8, 31, 136, 177
Hot Springs, 163, 166
Hudson Bay Company, 40
Hunter Act, 114
Hunting, 17, 19, 143-45, 152, 166, 179, 180

Ignacio, Chief, 103, 104, 114, 115
Ignacio, Colorado, 10, 28, 72, 104, 123, 160

Jack, Captain (Nicaagat), 60, 77, 89, 90, 92-95, 97
Jackson, Helen Hunt, 113
Jackson, Wm. H., 6, 10, 70, 71, 73, 138
Jicarilla (see Apache), 17, 28, 34, 35, 51, 60, 139
Johnson (Canalla), 77, 90, 91, 92, 159

Kearny, Stephen, 47
Kiowa, 17, 35, 56, 62, 133, 154
Kremmling, Colorado, 47, 89